GO BEHIND THE SCENES OF *LIVE WITH REGIS AND KATHIE LEE* AND FIND OUT:

- Why Kathie Lee has threatened to quit the show

- How Regis kept secret a serious heart problem that almost killed him

- Why critics target Kathie Lee and how she responds

- What fellow comics have to say about Regis

- Why hubby Frank Gifford wished Kathie Lee would stay home more

- How Regis and Kathie Lee's contrasting personalities create some of the funniest moments on television

- Their thoughts on each other

- And much more!

Books by Norman King

REGIS and KATHIE LEE

Their Lives Together and Apart

Norman King

St. Martin's Paperbacks

Published by arrangement with Birch Lane Press.

REGIS AND KATHIE LEE: THEIR LIVES TOGETHER AND APART

Copyright © 1995 Norman King.

Cover photograph by Photofest.

Library of Congress Catalog Card Number: 95-19246

ISBN: 0-312-96063-8

Printed in the United States of America

Birch Lane Press hardcover edition published in 1995
St. Martin's Paperbacks edition/September 1996

St. Martin's Paperbacks are published by St. Martin's Press, 175 Fifth Avenue, New York, N.Y. 10010.

10 9 8 7 6 5 4 3 2 1

To Regis and Kathie Lee
Thank you for proving that nice guys do finish first.

Contents

Acknowledgments

Thanks to Bill Adler, who directs my literary career.

To the talented and tenacious Bruce Cassiday, without whom my books could never have been written.

To Ron Konecky, the brilliant attorney who has always shared his natural kindness and an occasional Havana with me.

To Richie Friedman, the king of new issues, my friend, my guidance counselor, and my financial guru.

And, of course, to Barbara King: after forty years you still make each day a joy.

REGIS and KATHIE LEE

1

Regis and Kathie Lee as Cohosts:
The Dynamic Duo

The man paused to look down at a sheet of paper in front of him. Then he lifted his eyes to the television camera that was shooting him straight on and said:

"*Roseanne*—a twenty-nine share."

He was reading the Neilsen ratings for the New York Metropolitan area.

"*Jeopardy!*—a twenty-eight share," he went on. "*Wheel of Fortune*—twenty-four. *David Letterman*—twelve. *Jay Leno*—twelve."

He paused and took a good long look at the next one and then read it out in clear, ringing tones.

"*Live With Regis and Kathie Lee*" A three count. "Thirty-one!"

The audience broke out into loud cheers, with clapping and whistling surging underneath like a tidal wave.

The man was Regis Philbin, one-half of the redoubtable team of Regis and Kathie Lee. Seated beside him was his cohost, Kathie Lee Gifford. She was beaming.

"Gelman," he said to his producer-director, Michael Gelman,

seated off-camera to the right, "I don't think you should give me these things to read." And he began to laugh gleefully.

And the audience cheered all the louder.

On that recent Neilsen reckoning, *Live With Regis and Kathie Lee* had beat out all the competing shows even vaguely within their category—and they managed to do it in the New York Metropolitan area, one of the most lucrative markets in the United States. Even when the show did not outperform everyone else it came in consistently high. And the numbers were ever-increasing.

How come?

What could make people want to share their postbreakfast hours with an old, unreconstructed television talk-show rebel named, a bit dippily, Regis Philbin and a vital, somewhat conservative, avowedly straight-arrow singer and talk-show hostess named Kathie Lee Gifford?

There's no quick answer, no one-word explanation, no sound bite of instant clarification for this phenomenon. It's simply a fact of life. Perhaps, as one nonscientific viewer of this popular nine a.m. show has said, it might simply be because people *like* these two performers, whose lifestyles may be those of the rich and famous but whose attitudes and impressions of life are very close to those of the many millions of people who watch them.

One thing you always know about Regis Philbin and Kathie Lee Gifford is where each is coming from. Philbin honed his image through years of constant battle with network executives, ad agency bigwigs, and production chiefs. From the beginning he had the shrewdness to sense that he would always be exactly what he was when he began in the television business: the put-upon guy; the man Charlie Chaplin made into a figure of international renown; the comic that Buster Keaton played. Always a bit battered by life and the people around him, but never really a loser. A winded, reeling, amusing—say lovable—figure of a man who wants to win but can't always seem to manage it.

When a performer decides to imitate Regis Philbin, he or she simply puts on a tough look, lowers his or her voice an octave or so, and growls out:

"Get off my *case*! I can strike *back*!"

In spite of the threats, Philbin seldom does. In effect, in this age of female parity and sexual harassment lawsuits, Regis Philbin is the paradigm of the average frustrated American male. He is no matinee idol or TV favorite who kills off the bad guys with karate chops. Instead, he is the man usually on the run from the many (and sometimes imagined) evils of life around him. He plays the battered husband, the rejected lover, the last man to the finish line in an obviously rigged race.

In this way he builds sympathy for himself—and empathy.

Recently a great deal of hooplah centered around Philbin's cohost, Kathie Lee, who had accompanied her husband Frank Gifford to the socko premiere of *the* musical comedy supershow of the year 1994: *Sunset Boulevard*. As Kathie Lee, the morning after, was reporting all the excitement of the affair, showing film clips of her and Gifford arriving and chatting with television and show-biz notables, she stopped herself abruptly and gave Regis a mournful look.

"We didn't see you there." Then she sighed sympathetically. "Poor Regis—"

He cut her off with his patented growl and launched into a brief reminder that *Sunset Boulevard* had held its real opening night in London, had held a second opening in Los Angeles, and thus this New York opening was simply another performance of a long-running show.

Then Regis winked at the audience, indicating that it was all in fun, and the audience responded in suitable fashion. Kathie Lee got the point.

It is obvious that Philbin knows how to work the crowd. He had let Kathie Lee go on and on about her glamorous name-drop evening the night before; he had permitted the question to build in everyone's mind—Where were Regis and his wife during this gala function? He waited until it finally dawned on Kathie Lee that she was swanning all over the place and making her cohost look small and wasted beside her, and began pouring out her sympathy. *Then* Regis took her up, snapped at her, and put the situation into proper perspective.

At the same time, Kathie Lee was working her own side of the street just as skillfully as Regis Philbin. The fact that she had been name-dropping and one-upping him with all her might—without even realizing it—was simply a part of her personality. She also had the sensitivity to notice how quiet and subdued her partner had become. Then she turned into a sympathy machine. She brilliantly knows how to play *both* these sides of her character, and when to choose one or the other the moment she realizes where she is and what she is doing.

In many ways Regis Philbin *is* the male animal, and Kathie Lee Gifford *is* the female counterpart. The tension that works between them is a marvel to watch as they begin to play the oldest game in the world: the battle of the sexes.

Of course, any couple can play the game. From the days of radio, the morning chat has always been a viable and salable thing. Today, however, the team of Regis Philbin and Kathie Lee Gifford seems to be playing it with more skill and zest, and more dead-center targeting, than any other pair in the field.

While she is feminine and womanly, Kathie Lee is not a stick-in-the-mud. She does not suffer fools gladly, nor does she turn her back on a good argument. In fact, it was her quick retorts that brought her attention from the beginning of her talk-show career and almost sank her in the mire of the communications business before she even got started in it.

Kathie Lee has always been quick with a quip. Her wit may not have the grand complexity of Dr. Samuel Johnson's, but it is clean and precise. She knows how to use lip.

For example:

Every morning the cohosts of *Live* telephone someone out there to answer the trivia question of the day. It is a fixture of the show. Some of the people on the other end of the wire seem hardly awake. Others can't stop talking.

On a recent morning, one woman continued to talk and talk and talk long after Regis had almost given up trying to get her to answer the question.

When it was all over, Kathie Lee quipped: "She'll never be lonely. She'll always have herself."

That got a big laugh.

There was no need for any more verbiage on the subject. Regis went right on and the show continued. Kathie Lee had not let that nonstop talker leave without some kind of comment. It is small wonder that her autobiography, which came out in 1992, is subtitled: "I Can't Believe I Said That!"

Perhaps not. But the odds are that she *can* believe it; in fact, she *has* total control over her tongue and her brain and she knows when to use that lip of hers and when to keep her pretty mouth tightly shut.

Half the fun of tuning in to *Live With Regis and Kathie Lee* is the fact that you know you'll be getting strictly ad lib stuff. Nothing—except the cue card notes—is written up ahead of time. That does not mean that neither of the cohosts ever thinks of things to say in advance, but it does mean that the show is not structured to go down a single prearranged path. Where it jogs is up for grabs.

When you tune in you see the familiar set with the two of them sitting at their table. It is a comfortable, laid-back scene, with a staircase winding up behind them from stage left to stage right, and a clear area in front of their table. Always Regis sits stage right; Kathie Lee, stage left.

But today is a little different. Regis is wearing a T-shirt rather than a shirt, tie, and jacket, as he usually does. Kathie Lee looks at him somewhat questioningly, and he grins and says:

"I'm just preparing you."

"Me? For what?" Kathie Lee asks.

"For doing the show in the nude!"

She gives him a look. The audience howls with laughter.

But Kathie Lee has her moments, too. One day a group of four singers called Hootie and the Blowfish appears and does a number. They are dressed in ancient jeans and used-up sports shirts. Kathie Lee engages them in conversation. They admit it's not usual for them to be singing like this at nine o'clock in the *morning*. In fact, they make a big point of telling how hard it was to get up early enough to arrive at the studio in time for their stint.

Kathie Lee nods sympathetically, glancing over their tired attire. "And you had to dress up, too."

Big laugh from the audience. And the guests.

Regis can be quick on his feet, or in his special chair, too. It is the Monday after Notre Dame, Regis's alma mater, and Southern California have finished their football game in a tie. So Regis begins talking about the game. He cannot get it out of his head that tying a football game is a way of chickening out. Why not go for the win? Certainly with the two-point conversion, the last to score in a tight game can certainly *win* the game. Or lose it.

After some more discussion, which is like a monologue, Regis looks at Kathie Lee and says: "You know, kissing your cohost is just like tying a game in football."

It isn't always the two cohosts who provide the laughs. The production staff skillfully selects people with verve and a sense of humor to participate. They are mostly show business types, since it is their professionalism that makes them particularly palatable to an audience. They know how to work a crowd.

Timothy Dalton appears on *Live* to plug *Scarlett*, the TV sequel to *Gone With the Wind*, in which he plays the part of Rhett Butler (originally played by Clark Gable). He begins talking about his earlier work in the James Bond movies. He admits that the role of Bond was easy to do. Everything involved was weapons and costumes—not much stunt work.

8

Regis glances around the set and says, "You carried Scarlett up stairs just like those, didn't you?"

Dalton glances around. "As a matter of fact, I didn't. That was Clark Gable."

"What do you think?" Regis says, his eyes gleaming. "Could you—?"

The audience senses the challenge and begins cheering "Do it! Do it!"

Dalton stands up with a cool smile. "Who'll volunteer?"

"A very *small* girl," quips Regis, looking out into the audience. There is laughter.

A woman is selected, comes up and meets Dalton, and true to form he grabs her, cradles her in his arms, and begins to run up the steps. At the landing, he slows down some, and does the rest in a walk. He puts her down at the top, to cheers from the audience.

The two of them return downstage together. The substitute Scarlett disappears in the audience, and Dalton slumps into his chair. He is visibly winded and takes deep breaths to steady himself.

Laughter. No dialogue necessary.

Not all the gags are action bits like that one. Alan Alda is cohosting the show with Kathie Lee during one of Regis's brief vacation days. He keeps looking around the set and seems especially interested in the chair that Regis always sits in—which *he* will be using today. Finally he gets into it, squirming a bit at the tight fit. He looks at the camera and says:

"He's done very well for such a short person."

Big laugh.

Michael Douglas is doing a rundown one morning of some of his films, with Regis holding up stills of the shows. In his first directorial venture, Douglas made the classic film *One Flew Over the Cuckoo's Nest*, in which Jack Nicholson starred. Douglas points to a group shot in the hospital in which Danny De Vito appears. He calls him by name.

Several pictures later he comes to a shot of the *War of the Roses*, which was a direct turnaround, with De Vito directing and Douglas starring.

"You remember the climactic scene," Douglas says. "There I was high up on the chandelier, with Kathleen Turner just below me. It took a long time to get us ready for that shot." It was a dangerous one, too.

Then, just as the cameras were ready to roll, recalls Douglas, De Vito turned to him up there and grinned puckishly as he said, "Break for lunch!"

As the cast dissolved in laughter, Douglas continued, De Vito shook his fist at him and leered as he said: "I've been waiting a long time for that!"

Dana Carvey, substituting for Regis as cohost, does a number of imitations, including one of Frank Gifford: "Six times a day!"

When the laughter from that subsides, he does Bill and Hillary Clinton in the White House. "Our marriage just *sucks* compared to Frank and Kathie Lee's."

After entertaining the audience with tales of his working days—before signing up to do the television show *Wings*—Thomas Haden Church confesses that he had once worked as a scavenger for the state of Texas, down near the Border. In imitation of his redneck boss, he drawls: "Thar's a bloated goat lyin' on the highway. Been bakin' thar for seven days about." Pause. "Go git him."

His parting shot is right on target too. He shakes hands with Regis and with Kathie Lee and smiles broadly, as if for the first time understanding something about show business because of the sight of them.

"You know, the *good* thing is you don't have to be good-looking to be famous." Like us, he means.

But nothing matches the morning Regis Philbin comes in after seeing the premiere of *Disclosure*, the reverse sexual harassment picture starring Michael Douglas and Demi Moore. "What a great picture!" he enthuses, and then goes into a brief outline of the plot. It's about a woman who comes onto a man with whom she has had a previous affair, the same man whose promotion to vice president she has just intercepted for herself. Instead of succumbing to her, Douglas, a married man, breaks it off and leaves. Complications follow and Douglas finally charges her with sexual harassment—a 180-degree reversal of the usual situation.

Then, after the raves about the picture, Philbin leans toward the camera as if he were about to divulge important and confidential information. "I've got a little scenario of my own," he says, lowering his voice into its usual challenge mode. "My picture involves a man and a woman who are cohosts on a morning talk show."

People in the audience start tittering.

"The female member of the team secretly lusts for the show. She wants to be its single star. It comes to her how she can accomplish this. First of all she begins to get herself single engagements outside the show."

More laughter. Kathie Lee is giggling now. Regis and she have kidded each other about the fact that she has been getting more outside engagements than Regis has late in 1994.

Regis straightens himself in his chair. Still looking straight into the camera, he says: "I've got my eyes on you. Just watch out what you do around here. I know what's in your mind!"

Which brings up the point about Kathie Lee and her "single" engagements. Not only does she do shows in which she sings, but she makes record albums, and appears as a guest on other talk shows. Sometimes as a guest she will talk about personal things that are not the usual subject of talk-show guests. Or even her own show.

On David Letterman's *Late Night* show she becomes involved in discussing nursing her children.

"Nursing is God's way," she says, and proceeds to describe her physical condition during nursing. "I was engorged," she said finally.

Letterman is looking at the ceiling and elsewhere. The audience is laughing. Everybody knows his squeamishness about subjects of an intimate nature.

"But there's a way to avoid the soreness in the nipples," Kathie Lee goes on, totally ignoring Letterman's ravaged face—or, perhaps, deliberately exploiting his uneasiness. "I wore cabbage."

By now Letterman is speechless. The audience is intrigued.

Nothing deters Kathie Lee. She explains that she cut a cabbage in half, cooled it in the refrigerator, and wore the halves over her nipples. And that seemed to take care of the problem.

The audience applauds. Letterman passes over it smoothly. "I now have too much information about everything to do with nursing," he observes dryly.

The two performers—Regis and Kathie Lee—are brilliant foils for one another. Even though they have established themselves for a number of years as "Regis" (the put-upon one with the snarl and the growl) and "Kathie Lee" (the straight-arrow woman with the quick wit and the maverick lip) there are still occasional nuances in their give-and-take that makes their show a never-ending bouillabaisse of quips and snippets.

Take the so-called "Halloween Show" on October 31, 1994. With all the recent movies involving impossible physical changes— an old man in a young man's body, a man in a woman's body, a pregnant man, and so on—*Live* comes up with an interesting variation on the same theme. Kathie Lee becomes Regis Philbin, and Regis Philbin becomes Kathie Lee Gifford.

They stride onstage over the theme music. Their appearance is so startling that the audience has to mull it over and giggle nervously before really approving the scene.

Kathie Lee is dressed in trim black pants, a red jacket, and a man's shirt and tie. Her hair is a black wig, cut short, like a man's. She wears a stern no-nonsense look. She handles a bundle of cue cards, unlike her usual unfettered, empty-handed personage. She climbs into the chair at stage right and stares into the camera in a businesslike way.

Regis Philbin is cross-dressed as a rather buxom woman, with a light brown wig and makeup, not too heavy, but with obvious lipstick and eye shadow predominating. He wears a skirt and a white blouse over a foam-rubber bosom. He strolls onto the set with the flowing motion of a woman. He flashes a huge diamond on his hand—an obvious parody of the big diamond ring that husband Gifford gave Kathie Lee.

The show proceeds as usual, with Kathie Lee reading off the cue cards in a stern and challenging tone, and with Regis sitting beside him/her, smiling at the camera and flashing the huge diamond ring at intervals. At one point someone mentions the word "real."

"Real?" Philbin repeats. He flashes the ring again. "*This* is real. Nothing else in life is real. *This* is." And as for the Human Love Machine—"*He's* real, Reege!"

At another point he looks down at his hand and his face becomes contorted with pain. "Loose nail!" he cries in anguish, almost bursting into tears. He flips his hand in the air and shakes his head mournfully, trying to make the pain go away.

Meanwhile Kathie Lee is doing her Regis, imitating his swift, sure-fire manner. Nothing so much as a furtive smile crosses her lips. She is all serious and full speed ahead. She makes a mistake, reading from the cue cards, and immediately shrugs it off. "Who cares?"

As Kathie Lee continues to run the show, Regis leans back in his/her chair and gazes at that enormous ring, waving it in front of the camera. "I love this show!" he says, stretching back in the chair. "Nothing at all to worry about!"

Kathie Lee, suddenly out of character and definitely Kathie Lee, flashes him a nasty look and goes right on.

The following day, the two stars talk about the show and give their impressions of changing into one another.

Kathie Lee reports that Frank, her husband, thought Regis had "great legs." As for Kathie Lee, he thought that she "looked shifty" playing Regis. Regis, he told Kathie Lee, "seemed to be getting in touch with his feminine side."

TV Guide later comes out with a "cheers" for that show: "To the most hilarious drag show since Dustin Hoffman's *Tootsie*: the Halloween role reversal between the hosts of *Live With Regis and Kathie Lee*. Cross-dressed as Kathie, Reege cooed on and on about the Love Machine (the show's nickname for her husband, Frank Gifford). Meanwhile Kathie, made up as Regis, fumed and fussed about garbage trucks blocking the way to work and other mundane irritations. The show was a 'treat.'"

Comics come in singles, pairs, and triplets. Singles include Charlie Chaplin, Buster Keaton, Charlie Chan, and many others. There are fewer triplets or quartets than singles or pairs. The Marx Brothers. The Ritz Brothers. The Three Stooges.

The pairs spring to mind instantly: Laurel and Hardy; Abbott and Costello; Burns and Allen; Wallace Beery and Raymond Hatton. There are dozens of great teams.

The team concept works in comedy. One comic is always funnier than the other. The least funny member of the team is called the straight man. In vaudeville, where this kind of comedy developed, the straight man was frequently a woman. She appeared to keep the ogling eyes of the men in bald-head row glued on her. She kept the skit going, allowing the comic to go his way and carrying him when the laughter lagged.

To the average person it is the comic who generates the laughs. It is Lou Costello whose thoughts one follows by his facial contortions as he tries to puzzle out the "Who's on first" routine—probably the greatest in the history of comedy. Bud Abbott once laughed off that thought with an interesting comment.

"I never minded being the straight man," Abbott said. "After all, the straight man is worth more than the comic. It's the straight man who gets the loot—the highest salary. Why? Because he *carries* the comic."

In effect, the straight man is a substitute for the man or woman in the audience. He keeps the comic going so he and the audience can be amused at the comic's mad gyrations. Without the straight man to manage the timing and create the attitude, there is no humor to laugh at.

The question arises. Is Regis Philbin the comic, or the straight man? Is Kathie Lee Gifford the comic, or the straight woman?

It may be that the question was answered on that Halloween Eve performance when the two changed identities. For it was definitely Kathie Lee wearing male clothes and sitting in Regis Philbin's chair who played it straight and hard. And it was definitely Regis in drag as Kathie Lee who played it soft and comic.

And yet neither is either comic or straight all the time. The secret of their success seems to be that each can change from straight to comic on a moment's notice. And then switch back again when the gag is done.

Members of the audience empathize with both Regis *and* Kathie Lee because Regis is more than just the put-upon male, and Kathie Lee more than just the straight-arrow female. The secret of their popularity and their immense staying power is that the two of them share many *different* lives. Aside from the obvious fact that Kathie Lee is a singer and has been for years, Regis Philbin has been a show business star for years on his own as well as with Kathie Lee.

Between the two of them, they share lives galore. In order to understand these two people who come on every weekday morning at nine o'clock (in New York) to entertain you with their quips and quirks, it is necessary to know more about them and the struggles they encountered on their way up the very slippery and difficult ladder of show business fame.

2

Regis as Youth:
From Plebe to Patrician

It's very simple. If you ask Regis Francis Xavier Philbin who he is he will tell you: "I am the king." Not the King of New York. Not the King of Los Angeles. Just *the King*.

Back in 1988, when he returned triumphant to Los Angeles, where his career had previously fizzled in 1981, the now successful New Yorker stood on a chopper pad, high atop a luxury hotel in Universal City, and screamed, "I'm back, Los Angeles!" A helicopter hovered overhead, whipping the air about.

"The King is back! I've come to save you from boredom! No more snoozing at nine A.M.! The excitement is coming back!"

Today, at home in New York City, the location of his hit television show *Live With Regis and Kathie Lee*, he swaggers down the streets like a capo of the airwaves while construction workers hail him and pedestrians smile at him.

Finally, after years of playing second fiddle, Philbin is receiving the respect he so well deserves. As only he can tell you, cheers are a whole lot better.

Nowadays the King's ratings are *through the roof*, thank you. Not bad for the erstwhile whipping boy of Joey Bishop, the eponymous star of a short-lived late-night talk show that bombed in the late sixties. Exhilarated by his late-life success, Philbin keeps track of his ratings day by day in a near-religious ritual, making sure he is still securely seated on his throne.

Philbin was born in Manhattan on August 25, 1933, during the worst years of the Great Depression, the eldest son of Frank and Florence Philbin. His father was a personnel director, and apparently fared quite well, comparatively, during the depression years. At least he made enough money to send his son to Notre Dame, the college of his choice.

Regis spent his youth in the Bronx, where he attended Our Lady of Solace Grammar School and Cardinal Hayes High School. In fact, Frank Philbin had named his son Regis after his own alma mater, a Catholic boys' school called Regis High in Manhattan.

Philbin had a good solid family background. The families living in the Bronx during those years were very close-knit. There were lots of get-togethers with relatives. These generally turned into fullfledged "parties." They were what Regis remembers today as "family style" gatherings.

"We lived with my grandmother and my uncle," Regis recalled, "and the rest of the family lived upstairs from us, so there was a lot of dining with relatives."

Regis's mother was a great cook who distinguished herself in dreaming up marvelous Italian dishes. But she also knew how to prepare hams and steaks to make them tasty too.

Eating and having parties was all a part of his life then. That was long before television took over as the center of entertainment for the average "nuclear" family.

Dining was a lot of fun in those years. Nobody was health-conscious. Calories were known, but not printed in handbooks to carry around. And as a result, people enjoyed food far more than they do in the gloomy, weight-conscious 1990s.

A party in those desperate days of the thirties was, in effect, a family reunion of sorts—something for everyone to savor, recall in solitude, and look forward to.

Regis noted that his family still has those same kinds of parties. He described one as "a simple Saturday afternoon lunch with deli-type sandwiches and side dishes. The fact that it was a no-fuss lunch made it more fun, and we had more time for reminiscing."

And, happily, no time for TV.

School days for Regis Philbin were not happy ones. He was nominally good in his studies, but he never really applied himself. Also he was quite shy in school. Ingrown and introverted, he was hardly the type you would imagine would turn into the bumptious Regis of *Regis and Kathie Lee*.

The only time he ever seemed to perk up was in the years he began hanging out with his pals on the streets of New York. Then *nobody* could shut him up. Making wisecracks about people and putting bullies in their place seemed second nature to him. Here, he didn't have to study hard to find the best ways to do so.

A lot of people have tried to figure out exactly why Regis Philbin is the awesome comedian he is today. One of them seemed to hit closest when he zeroed in on Philbin's point of view and put a pseudoreligious spin on the man.

In a *New York Newsday* article in 1986, John Mariani observed that Philbin's Irish-American Catholicism reflected "the skepticism of the Jesuits in every joke he makes."

It is not difficult to detect this strain in almost everything Philbin says today, although of course he has tempered his style a great deal over the years and, indeed, honed an edge to it at the same time.

An underlying tone of "Oh, yeah?" can be found in every statement—and every gesture—that Regis makes. The bland skepticism is always there. Along with the hint that something is going on that is not quite kosher. When coupled with the eyebrow tilt and sideways glance, an almost bland statement becomes a devastating attack on a person, a thing, or an event.

What Regis Philbin learned on those street corners in the Bronx was to size up his confreres minute by minute in order to see if they were "in uniform," "in step," and "in good faith."

Then, if someone came up with a new cap, or a handkerchief that—God forbid!—had *initials* on it, he was fair game for a skewering. For the Jesuit in Philbin knew what was right and knew just as well what deviations were—well—*wrong!*

And, hence, suitable for torpedoing.

Regis Philbin still reads people with swift and cunning accuracy, which he first learned to do on that Bronx street corner in the late thirties and early forties.

It would have been a terrible shock to anyone to learn that Regis had gone to any college other than Notre Dame. Indeed, he did opt for Notre Dame, where he majored in sociology—as any good Jesuit might. He was zeroing in on science and the humanities, though he probably did not think of these as Jesuitical at all.

His college days were memorable. He was a student of sorts. But mostly he was a student of football—and Notre Dame had a good team in those years. Sports had always been a thing with him. He was basically puny, with a pixielike stance and a puckish grin on his face. Even in high school he had taken up weight lifting to develop his fragile body. And he continued to pump iron in college.

He felt he should go out for some kind of athletic team, and he eventually signed up for boxing. He did resistance training under the guidance of the gymnasium director, a Holy Cross priest named Father Lang. Philbin once described Father Lang as "the fourth-strongest man in the world." He did not name the three people ahead of Father Lang.

As for other extracurricular activities, Philbin did not bother.

He had always had a hankering to check out the campus radio station, but he could never work up the nerve to do it. He admitted later he had an overwhelming sense of fear that prevented him from getting what would have been his dream job—working around a local station.

"I just wanted to go inside and see what was going on. I walked over, but I could not bring myself to knock on the door and ask for a job to sweep out that station!" Philbin says. "So I never went in at all. That's how inhibited I was." He grins. "There was a little old lady who was the receptionist. Even years later, I'd go back to Notre Dame, and I was afraid to go up to her."

Maybe he was frightened that the crew would make fun of his name. Everyone else has done so, throughout his life and career.

"Johnny Carson has made great gags over the years about my name," Philbin told *Good Housekeeping* in 1992. "He said *Regis* was an English cigarette or a hotel. People still ask me, 'Is that your real name?'" A dumb question, Philbin blusters. "Why would anybody *adopt* a name like Regis Philbin?"

The foregoing must have been a patented Regis routine. Even Regis, for all his professed lack of foreknowledge, must have been aware of what life had in store for him. Plus, anyone with a smidgeon of Latin knows that "Regis" is the genitive singular of the word "Rex"—which means "King." He was going be *the King* someday. After all—it was written!

In January 1995 the *New York Times*'s humor columnist Russell Baker instigated a mock contest to search out names of contemporary celebrities whom Charles Dickens, with his propensity for naming characters for their dominant traits, might have used in a novel. The "contest" was judged by Baker in March 1995, and lo! in the Best List of Characters, Regis Philbin led all the rest!

Brenda M. Bergeron of Farmington, Connecticut, dreamed up "Sir Regis Philbin," labeling him as a "miserly, wealthy, despotic coal-mine owner." Frankly, the addition of "Sir" to "Regis Philbin" certainly has some kind of nineteenth-century ring to it, no matter what century he happens to be flourishing in—perhaps even the twenty-first!

During his years at Notre Dame, Regis Philbin the Real decided that he wanted to follow in the footsteps of the man he had come to consider his hero, talk-show host Jack Paar. Philbin knew he had a great gift for the old blarney. He fancied that he could interview with the best of them, and, as for monologues, who was a better monologuist than Philbin of the Bronx?

Philbin graduated from Notre Dame in 1953, with a B.A. in sociology, and spent the next two years in the United States Navy. Though the naval assignment was a good respite for him, what he really wanted to do was knock on doors and send resumés to all the radio and TV stations in the country.

In 1955, Philbin was out and back home. He knocked on doors and telephoned the brass at all the networks, but nothing happened. It wasn't until 1958, three years after his service in the navy, that he finally got his first taste of show biz. An uncle helped him land a job as a page on Steve Allen's *Tonight Show* at NBC-TV in New York. It may have been a remote connection, but it *did* get him in the business.

Three months later, at the age of twenty-five, he moved to Hollywood and commenced working for KCOP-TV, Channel 13, in Los Angeles.

"I started as a stagehand, a stage manager. Moving props, that sort of thing. It was very exciting. Channel 13 was all live. I drove a truck around town delivering film, parked the cars in the lot, and did all those little jobs," Philbin recalls.

"I also used to write critiques of Thirteen's programming and put them up on the wall. Real kid stuff. The general manager caught me and chewed me out. But two months later he gave me a job as Baxter Ward's news writer."

He worked a year and a half for Ward. But Philbin didn't want to work behind the camera; he wanted to move somewhere else to get his chance. Chucking his burgeoning writing career, he moved to San Diego, thinking he might get a job as an on-camera reporter. It didn't work out as he had hoped.

Instead he became a broadcaster in a mobile unit for radio station KSON-TV. "At six o'clock in the morning I was supposed to cover what was happening. The only things happening were a couple of drunk sailors staggering around. Maybe, if I was lucky, there'd be a stolen bicycle."

It took a while, but eventually he snagged a job at KFMB-TV, the local CBS outlet in San Diego. After working there as a newscaster, he moved over to KOGO-TV, the NBC station in San Diego. As part of the deal as anchorman, the NBC executives promised him his own talk show!

He stayed in San Diego from 1960 to 1964. *The Regis Philbin Show* was actually launched at KOGO-TV in 1961, true to NBC's promise. And so in 1961 Regis Philbin sat on his first talk-show stool and began a career of babbling about nothing of much import. This idle chatter would eventually become the trademark of his career and make him a superstar on *Live With Regis and Kathie Lee*.

Philbin couldn't have been happier. "It's funny. I [had] turned down a lot of anchorman deals because I wanted to be Jack Paar. Little did I realize that John Carson also wanted to be Jack Paar. And now the anchorman is king."

Philbin on the *Regis Philbin Show*: "Anyway, I loved that Saturday night talk show in San Diego. It was wild. The greatest talk show I ever had. Live, from eleven-thirty until one A.M. We had a studio audience, which was unheard of in San Diego in those days. It really caught on. We had all sorts of celebrities dropping in."

Philbin once tried to explain what he considered to be the origin of his talk-show style. "I had no tools to fall back on. I wasn't a comedian, didn't know any jokes. I still don't, really. I wasn't a singer. So all I could do was be myself and do what I did as a kid on the street corner. And I was a scream on the street corner."

To this day Philbin can still recall one memorable show in San Diego when Walter Winchell appeared as a guest. While

Philbin was doing the show, he noticed a host of policemen and firemen swarming all over the studio audience.

During the commercial break he learned that the studio had received a bomb threat, and that the police and firemen were there to look for the bomb. He reported this piece of news to the audience and told them that they could leave if they were scared.

What happened next is better told by Philbin.

"When the cameras came back on, some of them were heading for the exit. Suddenly, Winchell was saying: 'Wait a minute! Wait a minute! Don't let the ratskies scare you! These police and firemen will take care of things. Don't leave!' This one woman stops, looks at Winchell, and says: 'Walter, I love you, but I'm not going to go to hell with you.'"

And she didn't.

The show had been on exactly three years when Philbin got a call from Westinghouse. They wanted him to do a ninety-minute syndicated program they would telecast nationally from Hollywood. Philbin jumped at the chance to take a shot at the big time.

It was 1964 and he had become popular enough to replace Steve Allen on the Westinghouse talk show. He hosted the show from KTTV in Los Angeles.

Philbin's first guest was the astrologer Sydney Omarr, who told him on the air, "This show is not going to make it."

Not an auspicious beginning for Philbin's foray onto the glitzy Hollywood scene. Omarr pointed out that it wouldn't be Philbin's fault that his show would go down the tubes. Behind-the-scenes forces would lead to his demise. It turned out to be no idle prediction.

"He was right," Philbin said, recalling the incident. "There were a lot of shakeups and squabbles. I was not allowed to be myself on camera. But after ten weeks, the show seemed to have reached a calm stage and was gaining in popularity. So I got cocky. 'Bring Omarr back,' I ordered.

"And back he came. I admitted that much of his prediction had been correct, but that we seemed to have weathered the storm. 'I hate to be the bearer of bad tidings, but you're going to learn in the next forty-eight hours that your show is going off the air!'

"I couldn't believe it, but thirty-six hours later I got a call from the Westinghouse guys asking me over to the Beverly Hills Hotel. And I was out."

The show had lasted a mere thirteen weeks with Philbin at the helm. The memory still rankles. "That was my big shot, and I blew it." He goes into his put-upon spiel. "Merv [Griffin] followed me and *became a multimillionaire*! And I'm fighting with *her* [Kathie Lee Gifford] every morning! That's how *life is*!"

Not to be deterred, Philbin returned to TV soon afterward—the first chance he got—this time as a host of a weekly show on Channel 11 in Los Angeles. It proved to be a serendipitous occasion for him, because at that very moment a comic named Joey Bishop was casting around for an announcer for his new show, which would air on ABC-TV late night and go *mano a mano* with Johnny Carson.

According to Philbin, he and Bishop were naturals together. "We met and hit it off immediately. I was offered that job, and I took it. On the ABC network, but still up against Carson. I was what Joey wanted me to be—his announcer, his sidekick, his buffer. That's what he needed, and that's what I hope I gave him."

It may have been all peaches and cream when Bishop and Philbin started the *Joey Bishop Show*, but the combination soon turned sour, thanks to the show's poor ratings.

Philbin puts it diplomatically. "The show got off to a slow start and I began hearing from the ABC execs and people around Bishop that maybe I was the reason."

The fact is that Philbin wanted to be more than just a foil to Joey Bishop. He was not actually happy with the job of simply announcing; "I wanted to be known as more than just Joey Bishop's sidekick," he confirms.

On the show Philbin played second banana to a Joey Bishop whose main shtick was a very laid-back, deadpan wit. To play against Bishop's cool, Philbin had to act like an overgrown kid, full of youthful energy, gawking in awe at Bishop and his show biz pals who appeared every night. Each night Philbin had to introduce Bishop by hailing him as he privately gagged, "And now—twinkle, twinkle, it's time for Joey!"

Philbin found the whole thing a humiliation. But he played the role he was assigned like a trouper. Then, on July 12, 1968, he tossed away the script from which he was reading, and told Bishop to his face that he had heard rumors that the show was failing because of *his*—Regis's—presence.

"I explained . . . that I didn't want to come between him and success, and I walked off [the show]." Tears were streaming down his choirboy face. It was a very touching moment. Most of the fans of the show were quite moved.

Philbin even had a word for the reporters who next day covered the walkout in the newspapers. "It's one thing to lose your own show," Philbin said carefully, "but it's another to lose someone else's."

Always the laugh.

The executives at ABC-TV denied Philbin's allegations that they had plotted against him and were trying to dump him to save the show for Bishop. His statements, they said, "had no basis in fact."

In fact, they did not. Philbin never admitted it in public, but in truth Joey Bishop had suggested to Philbin that it might be an interesting ploy to pull a stunt like that. And Philbin agreed that it would give the show a shot in the arm—or at least a bit of publicity.

Which, of course, it badly needed.

It worked.

After his departure, a raft of letters swamped the network demanding the return of Regis Philbin. Bishop told his TV audience that night after Philbin's departure that he hoped his announcer would return to the series.

"Regis Philbin is like a son to me," said Bishop, very cool, very laid-back, very disingenuous. "He's one of the nicest persons I've ever met."

A week later Philbin returned to the show.

And that was the happy ending to Regis Philbin's first adventure in playing the prototype put-upon guy in public.

Philbin and Bishop have not spoken to each other in years, but Philbin cannot offer any explanation why. While on *Joey Bishop*, Philbin cut his one and only record album, *It's Time for Regis!* (which can now be bought on CD).

On the last day of the three-year-long, low-rated show's existence, Philbin hosted it and invited his old friend Sydney Omarr to predict the future.

"You know what?" Omarr told Regis. "You're going to become a household name, a very famous name."

Philbin was astounded. Also elated. "No kidding! Really?"

"But it's going to take time," Omarr warned him.

"Well, how long is it going to take? A year? Two years?"

Omarr smiled enigmatically. "Twenty years."

"Twenty years!" Philbin repeated, stunned. "*I'll kill myself*!"

The odd thing is, Omarr was absolutely on the mark.

Live With Regis and Kathie Lee went into syndication in 1988, or 1987. So it did take roughly twenty years, just as Omarr had predicted.

Meanwhile Philbin had married actress Kay Faylan, "a marriage that didn't work or last," according to his own analysis of the relationship. After eleven years, he couldn't stand it anymore and the two went their separate ways in 1968. At the time he was working on the Bishop program.

The Philbins had two children: Amy, now thirty-five, and Danny, now twenty-nine. Danny was born with missing vertebrae and no muscles in his legs. Later he was confined to a wheelchair.

He maintains that Danny is living comfortably in Van Nuys, a middle-class community where Danny interned in 1991 for California congressman Robert Dornan. Philbin says he talks to Danny every week by phone. "Every week," Danny concurs. "I love my dad, and I'm really proud of him."

While on *Joey Bishop*, Philbin met Joy Senese, who worked as Bishop's secretary-assistant. "She was always laughing," recalled Bishop. Philbin and Joy married on March 1, 1970. "I was glad that Regis was finding some happiness," Bishop said.

Philbin and Joy have two daughters: twenty-year-old Joanna, and nineteen-year-old Jennifer.

There was a lot of bouncing around for Philbin after the demise of the Bishop show between 1969 and 1973.

"I did *Philbin's People* on Channel 9—a talk show with people sitting around a table, relating to one another. Not bad. Then I agreed to go daily on a show called *Tempo*, where I worked for three years. Three hours every day, live, a lot of it without a cohost. I could do what I wanted.

"But no one ever watched Channel 9. It was like starting all over again. So I left there and hung around town for a year. Couldn't even get arrested."

But he did get jobs of one sort or another. He appeared in movies such as Woody Allen's *Everything You Wanted to Know About Sex*. In that film Philbin played a panel member of a quiz-show spoof called *What's My Perversion?* During the segment, host Jack Barry introduces the guest, a dignified-looking gentleman who "likes to expose himself on subways."

As a panelist, Philbin tries to uncover the gentleman's dirty little secret. Helping Philbin are his two fellow panelists Pamela Mason and Robert Q. Lewis.

"Do you need props?" Philbin asks the guest. "Is it self-contained?"

Philbin found his experience in moviemaking bizarre, to say the least. "Woody would stand around in his sneakers. I only saw the movie once, but I remember it as being pretty funny."

Years later Alan Alda was cohosting *Live With Regis and Kathie Lee* in the absence of Regis, and the subject of Woody Allen came

27

up. Alda had recently appeared in a new Allen film. He recalled that Allen actually never talked to anyone at all; there were no instructions from him as director. He simply let the actors work out what they would do.

"You know you're okay," Alda said, "if you aren't fired."

Philbin appeared in a number of TV dramas during this fallow period of his life. He remembers to his chagrin that he was "always cast as a reporter or television host. Even when I was on *Big Valley*, I was a frontier reporter. At least I got to wear a cowboy hat."

His career as an actor went nowhere. "Nothing out there but silence from the other side of the world. No one cares." He told a reporter interviewing him in 1980, "You're the only one who's called me in months. That's why I agreed to this interview, just to hear what it's like out there."

He even hosted two game shows in addition to his acting jobs. Nobody can remember the two shows, which were instantly consigned to oblivion. Philbin took no pride in either of them—*The Neighbors* and *Almost Anything Goes*.

Philbin described *The Neighbors* as a show in which "five neighbors from the same block were quizzed on how much they knew about each other." *Almost Anything Goes* was a type of *Beat the Clock*, which "required my presence in a lot of nice little towns in Alabama and Mississippi."

From 1972 to 1975 Philbin hosted a variety show in St. Louis called *Saturday Night in St. Louis*, thanks to his old friend Tom Battista. Regis was also hosting a boring three-hour morning show in Los Angeles, "fighting for my life," as he put it.

At that time Battista, general manager of KMOX (now called KMOV), phoned him from St. Louis and said, "Let's do something different. Something with personality—a live show. We'll fly you in."

Philbin and Battista had met in the sixties when Philbin was a news reporter in San Diego. Later Battista worked as his stage manager when Philbin did his own talk show there.

The moment Philbin received Battista's phone call about the

St. Louis gig, he was eager to get the show off the drawing board and into production. "This was the kind of show I wanted to do, winging it with a studio audience."

It proved to be a hectic schedule for him to maintain. While doing his L.A. job he flew to St. Louis once a month to work for a weekend in which he taped three or more shows and then did one live. He would arrive on Friday night and tape at least three shows on Friday, Saturday, and Sunday. He would perform the live show on Saturday night. After he taped the Sunday show he would fly back to Los Angeles, a physical wreck.

The show garnered such a huge following that Philbin got even less rest. They had him tape another half-hour episode that aired on Fridays at 6:30 P.M.

Even though he thought he would drop dead with exhaustion, he loved every minute of it. "I followed the Cardinals and I always read the local papers. I'd stay at Stouffer's [now the Clarion] and loved to have meals at the revolving rooftop restaurant, looking out at the city."

For the show, he interviewed any celebrity who happened to be on hand. As in San Diego he thought wrestlers made "great TV guests." One such wrestler, a four-hundred-pound Olympic champ called Chris Thomas, got carried away on the show and, after bruising Philbin's kidney, fractured several of the ailing host's ribs.

"I still can't stand up straight," Philbin informed a reporter the day after getting mauled by Thomas in 1973.

No matter. Philbin can't get enough of wrestlers on his show—to this day.

On the St. Louis show he did other stunts such as a demonstration of body painting with a drop-dead beautiful model. That wasn't all. On another episode he threw himself up to his neck in a mud bath with Betsy Palmer.

The series was broadcast at 10:30 P.M. and it regularly beat *Saturday Night Live*.

Battista recalled that Philbin's show "went through the ceil-

3

Regis as Performer:
Patrician to King

Ten years after leaving St. Louis, Regis Philbin returned in 1985. He had always enjoyed St. Louis, in part because it was in a St. Louis hospital that his wife, Joy, had their first daughter, Joanna, one weekend when he was working there on his television show.

Unfortunately, his return in 1985 was only a temporary thing. "I think I was there for a Variety Club telethon." He wishes even to this day that he could go back there again and stay in St. Louis a lot longer.

"I hear it's changed a lot—Kathie Lee said the city looked great." She had recently been there to promote a new line of clothes she was bringing out.

And Regis had always had a special dream about St. Louis. "I'd *love* to bring the show [*Live With Regis and Kathie Lee*] there some day."

With good reason. The St. Louis newspaper critics had always adored Philbin. The *Post-Dispatch* described him once as "a thirty-nine-year-old from the Bronx, dressed in mod clothes, wearing spitpolished Gucci shoes and beaming a boyish grin" and a "bright, articulate youngish top banana in Los Angeles."

After leaving St. Louis for L.A., Philbin bounced back and forth from one dead-end job to another. One of them included substitute hosting for Mike Douglas's syndicated TV talk show. It proved to be a disaster.

Philbin persuaded the producers to fly in wrestler Freddie Blassie, who had appeared on Philbin's former show in San Diego.

"Blassie was showing me some holds on the show. He had this beautifully coiffed hair, a nice pompadour that he had prepared especially carefully for this national appearance. As he was lowering me from a hold, I deliberately ran my hand through his hair. It aggravated him so much he chased me out into the audience.

"When he couldn't catch me, he returned to the stage and grabbed my jacket, which he proceeded to shred. I ran back, tried to get the jacket away, and he broke my finger. It's never been the same since. Boy, do I yearn for those good old days!" Not! Regis might have added.

Eventually, in 1975, he wound up as host of KABC-TV's *A.M. Los Angeles*, where he attained job security for a good seven years. There he honed his chitchatty, unscripted style of cohosting with a female partner named Sarah Purcell, who continued for four years. Cyndy Garvey took her place in 1979 when Purcell opted to leave the show and become a star on NBC's *Real People*. The show was live and spontaneous and showcased Philbin's sharpening talent at ad-libbing.

A.M. Los Angeles was a top-rated program and gave Philbin's flagging career a much-needed boost. *A.M.* dominated its time period. It even bested Phil Donahue's show when the two went head to head. *A.M.* even got better ratings than Johnny Carson in the category of female viewers between the ages of eighteen and forty-nine.

Philbin and his onetime producer Beth Forcelledo hashed out the format of *A.M.* Each episode started out with light banter between Philbin and cohost Garvey. Next came the trivia question, such as, "Who gave Deanna Durbin her first screen kiss?" Then came the first guest, audience call-ins, the second guest, more call-ins, the last guest, and final call-ins.

"And the answer is . . . Robert Stack!"

The basic format is close to today's *Live With Regis and Kathie Lee.* For example:

The list of guests included psychologists, celebrities, beauty experts, how-to authors, faddists, psychics, astrologers, gossip columnists, and nutritionists—all of them subjected to Philbin's quasibuffaloing manner of interrogation.

As for Cyndy Garvey, she appreciated Regis Philbin's "very supportive" attitude to her when they were off the air, but she began to find his on-air teasing just "a bit cruel." Finally, she felt it began "to cross the line of acceptability," according to an interview in *New York Newsday.* But she stuck it out. After all, the money was good.

As with Garvey, Philbin often found it necessary to defend his sometimes intimidating interview style. "I think it's necessary for me to keep them on edge. I can't just stand there with Mr. Fixit. I mean, something more than that has to be happening. So I have a little fun with them."

He was glad to be rid of his foil-to-the-master image. "The second-banana thing stuck for a long, long time, you know, and the critics kicked me around pretty good."

Still, Philbin was not all that thrilled at *A.M. Los Angeles.* After all, it was a local show; he wanted a national one. And when that break came in 1981, he decided to take a walk from *A.M.* The break was engineered by Grant Tinker, then chairman of the board at NBC.

Tinker asked Philbin to do a morning show on the network just after David Letterman's disastrous daytime show had unceremoniously failed. Even so, Philbin didn't get the whole hour he was originally promised.

Moments before the show was to start, he received word that the hour had been trimmed back to half an hour. Talk about a jinxed beginning! What's more, dozens of NBC affiliates refused to air the show, as they were still nursing a grudge against the network because of Letterman's heavily ballyhooed dud.

Yet the optimistic Philbin thought he had a good chance against Phil Donahue, who, for Philbin's money, was just a trifle too obsessed with sex.

"He's looking for the deviant that's even more deviant than the last deviant," Philbin said. "I am so sick of the sex thing. I just think it's been totally overdone. I caught a couple of sitcoms on the air the other night. They were all suggestion and innuendo. I know the guys who write these things. They just think sex is the most reliable way to get a laugh. Well, it's ridiculous. I hate it. I'm going to stay away from sex."

Well, maybe he *would* introduce it later—if his ratings plummeted. Which they did. Only by that time it was too late to introduce anything to salvage the show.

Philbin couldn't understand his lack of success. His favorite astrologer, Joyce Jillson, told him on the presentation tape that the show would succeed, as "Jupiter is going into Scorpio and Scorpio is the sign of the Nielsen."

Nonetheless, Philbin had misgivings about the show from day one. For one thing, he didn't like the title that the network came up with.

The truth of the matter was that he had absolutely no control over what his show was going to be called. What he wanted was a tricky one-word title that would catch the imagination and steer viewers to the show. Like *Today With Regis Philbin*, or *Tonight With Regis Philbin*. But of course those titles were already taken by someone else.

The TV moguls dreamed up some bizarre and, to Regis, idiotic things like *After Today*, *Later Today*, *Day by Day*. He was so exasperated with their lack of imagination that he went into his Regis Philbin act: "Hey," he said, his voice rising, "that's a *song*. Gimme a *break*!"

One morning in the NBC commissary Philbin met NBC chairman Grant Tinker. Tinker said, "Now about the title of this show—what does *Day to Day* mean?" He went on without waiting for an answer. "One thing I know about in this business is titles. I'm the guy who named it *The Mary Tyler Moore Show.* Remember?"

And so right off the bat it was Tinker's bright idea to call it *The Regis Philbin Show.* Well, what the hell. *The Mary Tyler Moore Show* succeded big, didn't it?

Philbin bowed to Tinker's superior knowledge and know-how. For that reason, the show would not be an ad-lib performance; it would be carefully scripted and taped in advance—like all the other late-night talk shows. It would be a new thing for Regis Philbin. He would sink or swim with it.

"I was Grant Tinker's first failure," Philbin told *Washington Post* TV critic Tom Shales, almost as if the fact was worthy of a prize of some kind. "I wanted that national break. Getting a call from Grant Tinker is like getting a call from God. When he came, NBC started flying, and everything they did was right. They had a terrific run. And I wish I could have been part of it."

With everything against it, *The Regis Philbin Show* died after five months. Philbin is convinced that the show collapsed so quickly because he had allowed himself to be talked out of doing a live broadcast in favor of doing a taped, scripted show.

He found himself yearning for his salad days at *A.M. Los Angeles,* where he could be himself and gripe about everything and everyone, including his bosses.

"They're really great, but sometimes. . . . They arranged for me to arm wrestle with the world's teenage woman champion. They set me up in this no-win situation. If you lose, you're a weakling. If you win, you're a horse's ass for beating an eighteen-year-old girl."

Apparently national exposure was not in Regis Philbin's future.

In March 1983 Philbin, forty-nine years old at the time, decided to switch from network TV to cable as a daily talk-show host for the Cable Health Network. He figured the show would be "good therapy" after his nationally televised program on NBC went down in flames. Embittered, he griped that he had not been "on long enough to attract an audience."

The gut-wrenching experience was enough to turn him sour over his television career. Disgruntled by the intransigent bureaucracy of network television, he was "anxious" to accept a job at cable when a onetime *A.M. Los Angeles* producer offered him a job on CHN. The producer was now a cable programmer and he wanted Philbin to host *Regis Philbin's Celebrity Health Styles*.

In many ways, Philbin was happy with the deal. For one thing, he had complete control over the product, a coup that was unheard of earlier in his career. He became the producer, the packager, and the host of the show. He called the hour-long program the "best show I've ever done."

The health show covered such topics as invisible braces and midlife crises. Philbin was actively involved in each interview. He engaged in physical demonstrations as well as in discussions with his guests. He had always been an apostle of physical fitness, and now he stretched with supple gym teachers and consumed protein-chip cookies that Lynda and Bruce Jenner, the Olympics decathlon star, cooked on the air. He permitted a dentist to stuff wax into his open mouth to determine whether his jaw was in alignment.

Other topics included a discussion of Ed McMahon's hernia surgery with McMahon himself as an interviewee.

Philbin was eager to please everyone on the show. "I've danced, jumped, jogged with them all and done whatever they've wanted me to do. But my favorite show was learning exotic sexercises with instructor Connie Cawfield."

Still, Philbin must have felt unsatisfied. It was a big comedown from network TV. Having had a taste of the big time, Philbin felt his talent was going to waste and his career was languishing in the cable boondocks.

"I have to be honest: it's disappointing not to be seen by as large an audience as I used to be." Worst of all, because his show wasn't carried in many parts of Los Angeles, "I can't watch myself."

Enough was enough. Philbin knew he had what it took to become a success. It didn't take a genius to see his career wouldn't amount to much if he didn't act decisively. In terms of audience numbers, cable would never come close to network TV.

Frankly, Philbin wanted as large an audience as he could get. Within months he made a decision to leave cable and, he hoped, to jump-start his stalled career. His critics at NBC be damned, he would hurl himself back into the cutthroat jungle of network TV with a vengeance.

In the latter part of 1983 he was offered a job hosting WABC-TV's local *Morning Show* in New York, a show familiar in format to *A.M. Los Angeles*. If he took it, it would mean pulling up stakes and heading east again. He decided that it was well worth the effort.

Morning was live and spontaneous and Philbin had a female cohost whom he already knew. She was his former *A.M.* partner Cyndy Garvey. He decided to take the plunge and see what would come of it. It was a risky ploy. Here he was taking charge of a show that had been a steady loser in the local tristate ratings competition for at least fourteen years!

However, within weeks, the show's Nielsen numbers rose from 1.0 to 3.0 in the New York, New Jersey, and Connecticut area. Cyndy Garvey quit to take on another assignment. Regis hired Ann Abernathy to succeed her as cohost. The upward pace continued. When Ann Abernathy left the show, Regis finally found Kathie Lee Gifford—then known as Kathie Lee Johnson.

In 1985 she joined the show and the ratings began to accelerate.

In 1990, Kenneth R. Clark wrote about the two of them in the *Chicago Tribune*. "He is a flamboyant vaudevillian who [affects] a curmudgeon streak that makes him the most prodigious complainer since Andy Rooney. She is impudent, irreverent, and possessed by an exaggerated sense of the ridiculous. They should have gotten along like King Lear and his more wayward daughter, but they didn't. They made chemistry."

By 1986, the Nielsen reports showed *The Morning Show* on 5.2 percent of the TV sets in the New York metropolitan area, was pushing *Donahue* (5.7) in popularity, and by 1987, the show had a thirty share of the tristate audience.

But Regis Philbin had not been resting on his laurels with only one show to his credit. From 1982 through 1987, he had been putting on one titled *Regis Philbin's Lifestyles*. It was actually a health show, featuring various diets, exercises, health tips, and the expertise of beauty mavens.

Regis did on-camera workouts with visiting exponents of physical fitness. Jack LaLanne and Hulk Hogan were two of his favorites. The show was broadcast on the Lifetime cable network. During its final months on the air in 1987, the show shifted to entertainers and aired under a different name: *The Regis Philbin Show*.

In turn, this gave Regis Philbin a lot more national attention than he had been getting with *The Morning Show*, which was strictly local.

In 1989 Philbin, undaunted as usual, began testing the waters of national broadcasting and found the answer when *Morning* went into national syndication with a brand-new name, *Live With Regis and Kathie Lee*.

And it was a marvelous deal for the two cohosts—especially for Regis.

It was the Disney company's Buena Vista that had taken a serious interest in syndicating *Regis and Kathie Lee*. By now, of course, Philbin was a veteran of the negotiations skirmishes that always occurred when a new show was proposed. He knew exactly what to insist on with Buena Vista—and he did insist on it.

What he did *not* want tampered with were the details of the format itself—especially the show's first seventeen minutes which had become known as the "host chat," where he and Kathie Lee ad-libbed their comments about the day's events and anything else that struck their fancy.

He made it perfectly clear exactly what he wanted, and said he would not go on with the negotiations until they agreed to leave the format exactly as it was.

The Buena Vista people said they would keep hands off the format and that there would be no tampering or "fine-tuning" by the syndication experts.

Regis was elated. At last someone had come along who could see the show for what it was and who liked it as it was—and not as it *might* be. There were, of course, some doubts about how the show would play nationally, but even Buena Vista took a chance now and then. It was a done deal.

In Los Angeles *Live With Regis and Kathie Lee* came on opposite, ironically enough, Philbin's old show, *A.M. Los Angeles*, which still aired on ABC-TV but with different hosts. Philbin's new show aired weekdays at nine A.M. on KHJ-TV, Channel 9.

Philbin was delighted to take on his old show as an adversary. "The good thing is that when you start with nothing, you can only go up. The force of viewer habit, years and years of watching whatever morning show they are putting on over there, is awfully tough to break."

"So I'm not expecting any overnight miracles. But I do expect some kind of reaction here in Los Angeles, and I can't help but feel some kind of rivalry with my old show." With the usual Philbin panache, he added, "I taught those guys everything they know!"

Walt Baker, KHJ's program director, was proud of adding Philbin to his morning lineup. "We believe we will be number one in that time period within six months, maybe less. Regis is a very recognizable commodity in this marketplace. He had a very large following, and I'm confident that that following will remember him and will tune in [to] this show."

KHJ launched an expensive ad campaign to publicize the new show, including full-page color ads in *TV Guide* that said, "Regis is back in the A.M., Los Angeles."

When asked if he felt threatened by Philbin's return to Los Angeles, the new host of *A.M. Los Angeles*, Steve Edwards, said,

"Regis who?" His cohost was Christine Ferrare, who used to be married to John DeLorean, the famous millionaire carmaker with all the legal bills.

"I'm confident we'll continue to do very well with the same thing we've been doing," declared Edwards. "I like Regis, and I'd like to see him do very well all over the country. But not so well here. There are always new threats. That's what television is about, and it probably will help get the adrenaline up a bit. But we still plan to go out there and win."

Since Philbin helped create *A.M. Los Angeles* as well as *Live With Regis and Kathie Lee*, the shows were identical, save for the hosts. *A.M.* even had Philbin's old producer from New York, Steve Ober.

From the start, Philbin expected his show to be the victor in his face-to-face combat with *A.M.* "Everything is already tried and tested and in place. We don't have to develop a new format or attitude or build a new set or find a new cohost. And what do I have to lose? Even if it bombs nationally, we'll still be a big hit in New York."

Well, it was a success. A big success. A monumental success. But slowly.

Philbin has strong opinions as to why his current show plays so well. "Everything on television these days is either written or overrehearsed and there isn't room for the smaller things in life that everybody goes through, like visits from your mother-in-law or the kids bringing home stray cats.

"TV usually thinks those things are too insignificant to be interesting to anybody. But that's all I've got. And it may sound a little hokey, but people relate to that, and they find those small little stories so appealing that they want to tune in the next day to find out what happened last night."

He went on, "This guy asks me why would anybody give a damn about what's happening in your life? And you know something, he's right! I don't know how to answer that question."

Philbin is best when he is just being Philbin. "That was my

hook from my early days in the sixties. That was the only thing I had and so I went with it—my reflections or my observations of what happened to me. I had no writers and so I had to rely on that real-life stuff, and that's become a trademark.

"It's just an ability to not only be honest but make that honesty into entertainment. You can tell a story about something that happened to you and it might be mildly interesting, or it may be wildly amusing. You hope to make it wildly amusing.

"If I have any ability, it might be that. It's to take those little mundane things and make them unusually entertaining and amusing to the audience."

On the other hand, Philbin is unsure why he and Kathie Lee Gifford are so much more successful than others in their field.

"It's hard to say exactly what our appeal is. I think people enjoy that opening segment. That's always been what people have remarked to me about. It's that opening exchange that I have with her and the audience and the television set. Hopefully, it's about what you've been talking or reading about."

He insists that the reason his previous nationally syndicated shows failed was because the producers refused to let him be himself.

"They'd say: 'But you can't do what you've been doing. We've got to change it. You can't go out there and talk for seventeen minutes without us knowing what you're going to say.' I always went along with them because they knew better, and it never worked.

"This time, when Disney wanted to syndicate the show, I said, 'Fine, but this time I'd like to do what we've been doing.' And I think I've proven the point."

Live With Regis and Kathie Lee was so successful in Los Angeles on KHJ-TV that in 1991 KABC-TV canceled *A.M. Los Angeles* and bought the syndicated production of *Regis and Kathie Lee*, which they put in *A.M.*'s place at nine A.M. weekdays.

Said Philbin, "I feel kind of vindicated. After going through all those formats to satisfy other people, it's this format, which I created, that's been the best for me. I'm proving it to myself and everybody else."

Even so, success did not come easily to Philbin. "My Way" may sound great in a song by Sinatra, but, "I wouldn't recommend it to anyone [else]," Philbin says. "It's been a long, hard, up-and-down trail. It really has. I wish I could have made it a hit the first time I did it. The thing is, always when I've had local shows, I made a success out of them."

Philbin revealed the secret of his success in five words to the *Montreal Gazette* in September 1991.

"I just wanna be me."

4

Kathie Lee as Singer:

Madonna of the Moral Majority

Like a scene straight out of a Jackie Collins steamy potboiler, Kathie Lee Gifford's first uncomfortable experience in Hollywood took place in a famous Hollywood player's car.

The man, who shall remain nameless, grabbed at Kathie Lee. She had just experienced harassment, Hollywood-style. Of course, she opted to continue leading the kind of spotless life she had always led.

Hollywood was a long way from the American Hospital at Neuilly, France, where she had been born Kathie Lee Epstein on August 16, 1953. Neuilly was a suburb northwest of Paris near the Bois de Boulogne and the obvious place for a serviceman in those postwar years to house himself and his family while serving his country.

Kathie Lee was the second child in the Epstein family. Her brother, three years older than she, was named David. Later on, a younger sister, Michele, would be born, also in France.

Her father, Aaron Epstein, was in the U.S. Navy. He had been posted in France to serve in the "occupation" army as part of the North Atlantic Treaty Organization, a military alliance established to protect western Europe from the cold war incursions of the Soviet Union.

Epstein had been a clerk for the Naval Academy Officer's Club in Washington before Pearl Harbor. He had signed up for the navy, eventually becoming chief petty officer. His father—Kathie Lee's grandfather—was a Russian Jew who had immigrated to America, where he fell in love with and married a Protestant woman.

In turn, Aaron Epstein had followed in his father's footsteps and also married a Protestant. In a religious sense, Kathie Lee's father was a nonpracticing Jew, who never interfered in the religious tenets of his family.

Kathie Lee's mother was named Joan Nancy Cuttell. "Mom is as gentile as you can get," Kathie Lee once said. Joan Epstein had had a somewhat miserable childhood, being shunted back and forth between warring factions of the Cuttell family. To her it was a relief finally to be married and settled down in a more stable atmosphere.

In April 1955, when Kathie Lee was twenty months old, her younger sister, Michelle Suzanne Epstein, "Michie," was born. During those first four years of Kathie Lee's life, the family was at the beck and call of the U.S. Navy, and moved first to Bremerhaven, Germany, and finally on to Chesapeake Bay in the United States.

By the time Kathie Lee was eight years old, her father had begun working for the Naval Research Lab in Washington. They purchased a three-bedroom Colonial house in Bowie, Maryland, a town northeast of Washington. It was there that Kathie Lee spent most of her formative years. As she told *Good Housekeeping* much later in 1991, "I had one of those glorious, radiant childhoods that I wouldn't trade for anything in this world."

Kathie Lee was a bright young girl who usually had all the

answers and was good at her school work. In fact, she was a National Honor Society Scholar with a grade point average of 3.9. Not bad for a child of the permissive nineteen-sixties! However, she was also amply supplied with a very competitive spirit. When she didn't win, she took it as a personal affront and tended to grouse over her loss, not in private, but in public—at least, to her family.

For that reason she had been nicknamed "Sarah Heartburn" by her siblings and parents. And yet such tempestuous times were rare in those halcyon days.

The atmosphere in the home was excellent, accounting for Kathie Lee's memories of a marvelous and sunshiny childhood. She has even referred to her parents as "Ward and June Cleaver crossed with Billy and Ruth Graham."

The reference to Billy Graham and his wife Ruth is not an accidental one. The family had been brought up Episcopalian, through Kathie Lee's mother, and Aaron Epstein usually accompanied them to church. However, he did celebrate typically Jewish traditions. "Bagels were a way of life for me," Kathie Lee has said.

The family was a tightly knit and loving one. Kathie Lee had no trouble making friends with her peer group in school. There were always people coming over to the house, with celebrations and parties galore among the kids.

It was a big deal for a teenager to have parties in the backyard, "but my parents never let us do that," stresses Kathie Lee.

Instead, her mother told her: "What I *will* do is let you have luncheons or dinner parties, and you will cook the food and set the table and pick the flowers."

Mrs. Epstein let her daughters use the best china, crystal, and silverware in the house to serve dinner parties, for four to six couples in the dining room. And she turned the entire management of each dinner over to her two daughters, with herself as supervisor.

The sisters served their favorite recipes. Then, when it came time for coffee, tea, and dessert, they moved their guests into the living room to sit by the fireplace. Kathie Lee says that this was her own favorite way to have her friends visit.

In that way, Kathie Lee's mother taught her how to entertain in a gracious way rather than just invite a bunch of people over to gobble pretzels and chips. She *could* have said, "Sure, have all your friends over, put them in the backyard, and we'll split for the evening."

But she didn't. Instead she told her daughters, "No, if you can't learn something from it, then you're not going to do it at all."

Kathie Lee recalls, "She taught me the importance of presenting a beautiful table, and planning a menu and a schedule of the evening's activities. I'm very grateful to her for that, because it required [her] involvement." And a deep involvement as well on the part of Kathie Lee and Michie.

The family did not confine itself to worship at the Episcopalian church exclusively, but sampled all varieties of Protestant sects in a hit-or-miss fashion. And so it was somewhat of a shock for twelve-year-old Kathie Lee to arrive home one evening and find her younger sister Michie, then ten, and her mother seated in front of the television set, stunned, red-eyed, and wailing.

Even more peculiar was the *reason* for this agnostic pair's tears. They had been channel-surfing from spot to spot when they had tuned in on part of a Billy Graham crusade. The family had watched Billy Graham for years, making cool and calculated comments about what he was saying and what he was doing. So far, nothing had taken root in their minds.

What had happened, Michie told Kathie Lee, was that their mother had fallen down on her knees in front of the television set and asked out loud for the Lord to come into her heart. And then, Michie confessed, she herself had gone down on her knees as well. During this confessional, Aaron Epstein suddenly arrived home for dinner to find the family in this entirely new emotional state.

Joanie Epstein was "born again," she told her family without shame or embarrassment. Shortly after that, Michie said that she too felt the same way. Soon enough Aaron Epstein announced that he had been thinking it over and he had decided to join his wife and daughter and rededicate himself to the Lord.

And very soon afterward, of course, Kathie Lee joined the rest of them. It would take her brother David a few years of living as an agnostic, but in the end he too would take the same path and become a Protestant minister.

Kathie Lee was to learn later that her mother's conversion had been prompted by a secret guilt that she had nourished in silence over the years. It turned out that in 1957, two years after Michie's birth and four years after Kathie Lee's, Joan Epstein had had an abortion in order to avoid bearing a fourth child.

When Kathie Lee learned of her mother's abortion, she did not judge her in any way. "The one thing that suffering should do for a person is to make you compassionate," she said.

At first, the actions of her immediate family caused conflicted feelings in Kathie Lee. She knew her mother and sister and father were sincere in their religious selection, but somehow she could not really make any kind of commitment as yet. It would be only a matter of time. Meanwhile, frustrations, doubts, and traumas all worked at her persona.

In a larger sense, she was caught up in an international revolution of moral precepts. The permissive nineteen-sixties had shaken the world. Almost every country was experiencing an opening up of ideas, of hopes, of dreams. Old inhibitions were being thrown out, old-fashioned ideas jettisoned, new ways tested.

She recalled that as a teenager she was forced by her peers to choose which moral course she would travel and which political position she would select to follow. However, since neither extreme of the political spectrum seemed at all feasible, she simply opted out and chose not to elaborate her position. Besides, she knew that once she had decided, the side she chose would own *her*. And she was too independent for that!

On a smaller, more intimate scale, Kathie Lee was facing another kind of revolt: that of her own body. She was in her teens now, trying to understand and cope with the maturation process. And, as usual, she was working at it with the sense of competition that had always been central to her personality.

She took up cheerleading at high school. She liked being in front of the crowd and encouraging them to scream and shout for action on the football field. And at the same time she realized that she loved to sing folk songs for Veterans Administration functions. Both she and her sister Michie were natural singers. Yet Michie had range and depth and an ability that was unmatched in Kathie Lee.

For the Epstein sisters to be interested in music was not surprising.

"My dad was a jazz saxophonist, and played with a group called the Five Moods," Kathie Lee told the *New York Times* in 1991. "And my mom sang on the radio."

Her father loved jazz, and could play it as well as he could play ordinary pop and classic. Music in the Epstein household was a real live thing. Kathie Lee and her sister Michie grew up knowing all the current Broadway musical scores almost by heart.

Kathie Lee has often told the story of her crushing experience with her sister Michie's vocal coach. The coach went through a number of exercises with Kathie Lee; finally the teacher leaned back and folded her arms over her chest. It turned out that Kathie Lee's total vocal range was about seven notes—at the most. "Kathie," she said with a vague smile, "stick to harmony."

Despite the painful put-down, within three months Kathie Lee found that she had won the talent award from Bowie's Junior Miss Pageant. Later, she went on to win the Maryland Junior Miss Pageant as well. And that in turn allowed her to take part in the national contest, which had as one of its judges a favorite of Kathie Lee's—Anita Bryant.

And that interesting turnaround taught Kathie Lee a lesson she never forgot. The lesson had to do with talent and persistence. Talent, she realized, was a commodity that was all over the place.

Many people had it. But of those who had it, few reached the very top. The ones who did always seemed to have one other personality trait that was rarer even than talent. And that quality was persistence.

If Kathie Lee had not persisted and gone right ahead with her singing, in spite of the musical coach's suggestion, she would have been left by the roadside, a disappointed and frustrated nonsinger. Something inside her had rallied to the cause and made her try that much harder to do her very best. Although her talent may have been lacking in certain finer points of artistic craftsmanship, her persistence had made what she did have pay off for her.

The lesson was never lost on her. It became a centerpiece of her character from that day on.

But, getting back to Anita Bryant. . . . The questionnaire that Kathie Lee filled out for the national pageant to be held in Mobile, Alabama, contained one pertinent question: "What famous person would you like to spend an hour with?"

Kathie Lee knew exactly—Anita Bryant, the singer and performer. In a way, Anita Bryant was a kind of heroine in the Epstein household. She was a favorite of Joan Epstein's as well as Kathie Lee's.

Joan Epstein had once told Kathie Lee that Anita Bryant was a Christian in the world of show business, where it was difficult to be one. Unfortunately, it would come about that Kathie Lee's pageant experience was basically a negative one.

The judges disqualified her from competition because she was caught talking to a young man on the pageant staff. Kathie Lee had been unaware of the rules: hobnobbing with boys was prohibited under the strict rules of the contest.

But there was one more surprise waiting for Kathie Lee in Mobile. One of the most enriching prizes at the pageant each year was the Kraft Hostess Award, presented annually by Kraft Foods. Each contestant is required to plan an entire party for guests—complete with invitations, decorations, menu, and games to fill in the time.

Kathie Lee had always enjoyed this kind of activity. (As she told the *Orlando Sentinel* later on in 1994, "I do *love* to cook. I like to do pasta. I just don't really have a lot of time anymore. Plus, I get fat if I eat it.") She put all her creative energies into what she called a "Hang Ten" luau—a combination of surfing lingo and Hawaiian fish fry.

After being washed out of the competition proper, Kathie Lee won the Kraft competition hands down—winnowing out a $1,500 scholarship and a contract to film a Kraft commercial.

So, even though she had lost the main event, she had come out a winner in one very nice aspect of the pageant.

There was one more bonus. Backstage just before the final broadcast of the pageant, Kathie Lee found herself in conversation with Bob Green, Anita Bryant's husband. It was one of those casual chitchats, with Green simply making small talk. He asked her if she was planning on going to college in the fall—which all the other contestants obviously were—but Kathie Lee admitted the truth. She wanted to get a job at Disney World.

"Maybe Anita and I can help you," Green mused.

"It'll have to be after June," Kathie Lee said. "I'm going to Israel with my mother for the Jerusalem Conference on Biblical Prophecy."

Green stared. "You are?" He grabbed her arm and dragged her over to Anita Bryant's dressing room.

"Anita!" Green said. "The Lord has answered our prayers!" Both Kathie Lee and Anita stared at him as if he had lost his mind. "We've got a baby-sitter!" The Greens, it turned out, were booked for the same conference.

Kathie Lee was not called upon to use up much of her Israel time baby-sitting, but she enjoyed such good rapport with Anita Bryant and her husband that when they returned to the United States, she was hired by Anita Bryant to sit for the four Green offspring in Key Biscayne, Florida. She also did odd jobs for the Greens.

She worked there for about a year. It didn't take much time

in the Green household for her to become a true born-again Christian. And her gospel singing improved significantly. She found herself much more self-confident, aware of what she was doing when she was singing, and managing to project her straight-arrow personality out into an audience and over the air waves.

Then one day one of the composers and arrangers took her aside for a little advice. What he told her was that she was a talented singer. She had a fine voice that she should use singing for the Lord. But he warned her that she was in danger of losing track of her own direction. She should go away to college and find herself musically. There was a short pause, and then he added: "You sound too much like Anita."

At one time sounding "too much" like Anita would have been a compliment to Kathie Lee. But now it actually wasn't: She had been missing something from her life. Where was her vaunted creativity? Where did her future lie? Sure, she could go on singing gospel all her life, being an Anita Bryant II, she knew that, but was that enough?

She was all mixed up. Her relationships with men were difficult. And she was having an identity crisis. Her analysis of it went like this:

She was not growing into the kind of woman that God wanted her to be. Instead, she was simply becoming a poor carbon copy of a true original. More than that, she realized that Anita was the basis of the problem. Her close relationship with Anita was stifling her own growth into the real adult Kathie Lee. She had to leave and try to find herself spiritually, emotionally, and musically.

There was more to it than that.

She realized that she had simply traded mothers. She had left her own mother and was now listening to another. She had to get her youth back and mold it the way she wanted it to be while she was still in control.

And there were still other considerations. Living with the Greens, Kathie Lee had come to realize that what looked good on the surface was not necessarily good on the inside. The marriage that looked like one made in heaven was a delusion. She saw it immediately when she had settled in with the family at Key Biscayne.

She said nothing, of course, as was her way with things that were unpleasant. Later on—in 1992—she opened up to *New York Daily News* writer Glenn Plaskin. "Anita was my friend," she said, "but her marriage was a sham and her children suffered from it. Yet on TV commercials, they looked like the perfect American family. What I saw of her life, I didn't want."

She had to leave Florida. Much as it hurt her to break up with Anita Bryant, she felt she must. And then Anita Bryant, suspecting what was worrying Kathie Lee, came to her rescue. At the time, Kathie Lee was busy with the work that had accumulated on her desk when the door opened and there Anita was. What startled Kathie Lee was the fact that she had tears in her eyes.

"Kathie," she said. "I just talked to Oral."

Who was Oral? Kathie Lee asked.

"Oral Roberts," Anita explained. And then, according to Kathie Lee, she laid it all out for Kathie Lee, just the way Kathie Lee would have wanted it. "He says you can come out to his college in Tulsa, and they'll make all of the arrangements for your admission. You start in two weeks!"

But what were the tears for?

"We'll miss you," Anita Bryant said, hugging her.

And indeed two weeks later Kathie Lee Epstein was in Tulsa, Oklahoma, enrolled as a freshman at Oral Roberts University— known familiarly as "O.R.U."

It was not, as Kathie Lee later told a friend, a university that could easily or accurately be described. Physically, it was a marvelously scenic campus comprising five hundred acres of lush green prairieland. Emotionally, it was a family, an education, and a fellowship all rolled into one. It had to be lived to be understood.

And yet, in spite of its beauty and its companionship, it was an ordeal for Kathie Lee. Here was a university dedicated to the spirit of fundamentalist Christianity. And here was Kathie Lee

Epstein, whose name was instant proof that she was hardly your garden-variety Christian. She was feeling a deepening reluctance to tell anybody her *name*.

Frankly, she was growing unhappy about being herself. She later recalled that she began to dislike herself, and as a result had a great deal of trouble believing that God liked her. As for the other people at Oral Roberts. . . . Well.

Only weeks after she had enrolled at O.R.U., the president of the university called her in and asked her to sing in chapel at a special service. George Wallace, the governor of Alabama, had been badly wounded during a political rally in Maryland. Naturally Kathie Lee agreed to do so. After all, she was getting her education on a singing scholarship. But she could feel that dreaded fear of exposing herself to her fellow students too quickly, too soon.

A special telephone hookup was established between O.R.U. and Governor Wallace's mansion in Birmingham, Alabama. The university president then introduced Kathie Lee to the student body and to those listening in Alabama with all the stops pulled out: Anita Bryant's help in getting her placed there; the money she had won at the Kraft Hostess Award; her singing ability, and so on.

She stood there stripped of her protective façade. There was no mystery about her at all. She felt alone and betrayed. Vulnerable. Targetable.

But then, as she began to sing, all those feelings of negativism vanished. She later said that she learned a big lesson that day.

"I am who I am. I am what I am because of who I was yesterday and all that I have experienced until today." The best thing to do is "accept your past in any way that you must in order to justify its presence in your life right now. Only then will you be truly ready to face tomorrow."

Her identity crisis, which had been a monkey on her back for some time, seemed finally to have been resolved. She was Kathie Lee Epstein—always had been and always would be.

Although she may originally have been intimidated by attending Oral Roberts University, she made the most of it in the two full years that she was there. Probably her most enjoyable experience at school was her two-year stint in O.R.U.'s World Action Singers. This was a participatory performing experience that provided scholarships for needy students. Each year six men and six women in the college traveled and sang on television and in public for Oral Roberts University.

For Kathie Lee, World Action gave her an opportunity to develop as a performer. Frequent trips were made to Hollywood for taping and performing sessions. She was able to meet a number of people in the entertainment world, as well as talented professionals working with O.R.U.

Her sense of competition was stimulated by her daily association with other professionals. "I learned . . . not to be satisfied with anything less than my greatest performance; that way I initiate a constant challenge to do better the next time around."

In her second year at O.R.U., Kathie Lee persuaded her sister Michie to enroll. It was during Michie's first year at O.R.U. and Kathie Lee's second that Kathie Lee came up with an idea. She and her sister would make an album together. They would call it *Kathie and Michie: Friends*.

There were a number of reasons that Kathie Lee decided that she simply had to leave Oral Roberts University. She thought the World Action ministry was a marvelous thing, but she had begun to feel her effectiveness could be enhanced if she were no longer at school. She had made friends with the television camera, but it was a sorry substitute for the warmth and energy she had felt from ministering to an audience of real live people.

She was afraid of losing contact with the needy world that lurked out there behind the bright lights and cameras. She knew she had to leave O.R.U. and the World Action Singers before she lost the connection altogether.

Later she gave *People* magazine a slightly different reason for leaving. "They tried to cookie-cutter all of us," she said of her college faculty. "I wanted the diversity of life. God went to the trouble to make us unique. They wanted us to believe the same way, think the same way."

It was 1975. Kathie Lee Epstein was not yet twenty-two years old. She knew she was an anomaly. The sixties were over. The world was well into the seventies. Kathie Lee had not joined the sixties revolution.

Yet because of her belief in God and her stubborn nature, she had not given in to the quick fixes of the time, nor for the instant gratification desired by so many. She had, in fact, remained a virgin in a world where that word and that fact had become things to be amused at and almost derided.

Yet it was time to make another significant turn in her life. She had studied communications, drama, and the arts at Oral Roberts University. Why shouldn't she succeed in the real world out there? She had met performers in music and theater in Hollywood. It was time to make a move in that direction; she knew that was where her future lay.

And so in 1975 she made the odyssey from Tulsa to Los Angeles, flying out to L.A. on March 19.

5

Kathie Lee as Newscaster:
"Is That All There Is?"

It was a wrenching thing for Kathie Lee Epstein to pull up stakes in Oklahoma and make a move to Los Angeles, California. Her first days on the West Coast in March 1975 were not exceptionally pleasant ones. And yet she did have friends who put her up—at least for the time being.

Soon she was involved in the rat race that envelops many upcoming show business people. Auditioning for commercials. Singing for record company moguls. Recording gospel albums. Trying out for acting parts in the soaps. Doing the thousand and one things every aspiring performer has to do to get started.

Mostly she was eager to shed her reputation. She knew what others thought about her. She knew she did not really belong to the sixties—which were gone now anyway. But she no more fit into the seventies than she had into the sixties.

In an attempt to set her thoughts about herself into some kind of order, Kathie Lee sat down and started to put those ideas into words. As she wrote, the words continued to come. And before long, she found she had amassed a great deal of data about herself and about the world around her.

"Today's youth wants answers," she wrote. "They are no longer satisfied with their parents' evaluations; they want to find out for themselves. I know because I, too, am young, grew up in the church, and have had to face the incredible pressure to join the 'revolution generation.'"

She went on describing the conflict in most young people between traditional values and the "new morality."

"I, too, have experienced change in many directions during my twenty-two years. Most of it has been exciting, much of it has been frustrating and disappointing, but *all* of it has been frightening!"

She said, "My life has been more riotous than revolutionary—a 'quiet riot.'"

As she wrote those lines, she realized that she had stood against the general permissiveness of the sixties and in doing so had become something of a figure of respect to her elders. She continued to write down her views of her spiritual life, until she had finished a book-length treatise.

Encouraged by her peers, she sent it away to a publisher and forgot all about it. In 1976 the book came out. Titled *The Quiet Riot*, the publishers paid her ten thousand dollars in royalty advances. Not bad for a young woman of twenty-three years who did not even have a college degree!

Life began to move faster for her. Within a year after arriving in Hollywood she had met, fallen in love with, and married a man named Paul Johnson. He was a blond, blue-eyed gospel composer. To her, Johnson was "the ultimate Christian catch."

They celebrated their wedding in 1976 in Acapulco, where, to her misery, she found out how wrong she had been about him. And about marriage. The two of them partied with reckless abandon in the Mexican resort town, but they did not seem to be able to relax with one another. Kathie Lee could not bear it.

In her view, her marriage dragged on for years. She could not bring herself to divorce Paul Johnson. After all, it went against the principles that had always dominated her life: the principles that had made her what she was and perhaps had militated against a successful marriage to the man with whom she had fallen in love.

"It was a real disappointment to me, as I know it was for Paul," she said in 1992. "We all want to love and be loved, and when it doesn't happen, it's devastating." The problem was that the two of them had saved themselves "for so long and expected it to be so good because we had done it 'right.'" Their relationship was a debacle. "It was not passionate, and it was not successful, but it was polite."

Hardly the thing a young bride longed for on her honeymoon.

The agonizing ordeal of her marriage reached its nadir after six long years. Ironically enough, as her marriage hit the skids and withered, her career as a gospel singer, as well as Paul Johnson's as a composer, flourished. Each of them became a hot number in gospel-music circles.

Now going on twenty-five and buoyed by her successful career, Kathie Lee in the 1977–78 season branched out into another area of show biz, that of the "La-La Lady" on the quiz show *$100,000 Name That Tune*. She was called the "La-La Lady" because she would sing "la-la" instead of the actual lyrics of the songs. She worked for a full season—taping twenty-six episodes for Ralph Edwards Productions.

On a roll now, Kathie Lee landed a job as a "Hee-Haw Honey" on a spin-off of the original *Hee-Haw* TV show, which used to feature country singers and down-home humor with the likes of Johnny Cash and Merle Haggard.

But even her skyrocketing career wasn't enough to compensate for her dying marriage. That fiasco concluded in 1981 when Kathie Lee returned home one day to find that Paul Johnson had moved out. It was one of the all-time lows of her life.

In point of fact, she felt insulted. "At the end of my marriage, I felt like I had presented myself as a gift to my husband that had been given back." What was the problem with her? she wondered. Wasn't she good enough for Paul Johnson?

On the other hand, she now believes that divorce was the best thing that could have happened to her. The marriage had been a mistake from the beginning.

"When I was divorced," she explained in 1992, "my foundation was ripped out from under me. I spent about two years being very lost. I had always been a strong person, capable and confident, but divorce was devastating."

She explained. "In the world I grew up in, divorce is not an option. You stay married, you work out your fights and your battles, and you pray."

Her world had crumbled away from her. "I had no direction. I was . . . dating. I was in relationships that were destructive, trying to be loved because I'd been so rejected. Maybe this person will love me. Maybe that person will love me."

In any event, six months after Kathie Lee's marriage to Paul Johnson was over, *Good Morning America* asked her to do field pieces for the show. The twenty-nine-year-old reporter moved to Manhattan in June 1982 to accommodate the program. She rented a basement apartment on the Upper West Side and substituted for Joan Lunden on the morning talk show.

It was on the set of that show that she first laid eyes on Frank Gifford, an ex-football great and at that time a television sports commentator. He himself was filling in for the star of the show, David Hartman. Kathie Lee's first sight of Frank Gifford was his backside. He was busy inserting his contact lenses in front of a mirror. It was the sight of his "incredible set of buns" that caught Kathie Lee's eye.

Immediately she knew that this was the man for her. Actually, she had not been living in a nunnery after her divorce from Paul Johnson. Among the men in her life was banker Stan Pottinger, an erstwhile boyfriend of Gloria Steinem's.

"I did live a very full life before Frank," Kathie Lee has confessed.

After clapping eyes on Frank, she could not stand being away from him for long periods. It was only a matter of time before he would be hers in marriage.

As it turned out, the marriage occurred on October 18, 1986. She was thirty-three years old; he was fifty-six. Kathie Lee has never had a regret that Frank "is a traditional guy, and his attitude was, 'You're mah woman.' Some women regard that as a Neanderthal approach and find it appalling. I found it appealing and sexy."

To this day she can't wait for him to return to their home after one of his television forays out of town on *Monday Night Football*. "I fully intend to be bubble-bathed with candles lit. Who knows *what* condition he'll be in. A girl can only hope."

It was about this same time that Kathie Lee came to the attention of Regis Philbin, who had his own morning show in New York, but liked to watch her on *Good Morning America*. Enamored with her in a professional way, Philbin suggested she join him as cohost on his show.

"She makes David Hartman look like a young guy," recalled Philbin. He hoped she could do the same for him. He was fifty-nine then and wanted to look thirty-nine.

Philbin brought Kathie Lee to his show in 1985, and the rest, as they say, is history.

Although he cannot actually put his finger on any one element of her personality that has made her the tremendous success she has been on his show, Philbin lays much of it to that tiny but tough slice of chutzpah—gall—lodged permanently in the heart of her character. In spite of the fact that she's got oceans of feeling and emotion inside her, it's the chutzpah that makes her totally unafraid to express herself in any way she chooses.

Regis senses that there is a war going on inside Kathie Lee. It's the chutzpah battling against those softer empathetic emotions. One moment the chutzpah will win out; the next, her sensitivity. The contrast makes for quick twists and turns—and brings on laughter from all those viewing and listening to her. The secret of her comic shtick is that you never know which side is going to surface—nor, for that matter, in what manner that winning side will express itself.

As for Kathie Lee, she has never had any qualms about her phenomenally successful career that began heading for the top at just about the time she joined Philbin's show. Because she had always been a hard worker and had never given up her desire to excel in show business, she feels that she deserves all the rewards she has gotten—the family she now has, the glory she has attained, and the money she controls.

"I never feel like 'How did I get here?'" she told the *Hartford Courant* in 1992. "Because I remember every time I sang, every time I had to go on an audition, every time I flew all night to get somewhere only to be told—'Ooooo. We're not looking for you at all.' You pay your dues in this business. Unless, of course, you're Vanilla Ice."

She went on, "There's a part of you that's extremely rewarded on the one hand because you think: 'Finally! Somebody gets it.' And another part of you that feels guilty about it because people are hurting in this country so much right now."

Indeed, there are times when she feels awkward doing her show with Philbin. A case in point: "When we had Desert Storm I really felt very awkward coming on in the morning and doing our show. . . . It makes you feel extremely shallow and selfish when people agree to putting their lives on the line and you're talking about what restaurant you went to last night. I mean, it's a fine line on our show anyway."

Philbin has nothing but awe for her talent as a talk-show host. "She's a fascinating character. There are a lot of different people there. What you see is what you get and they're all Kathie Lee. But what drives her is the key question I don't have a definitive answer for."

Kathie Lee isn't sure what drives her either, but she knows she is a bundle of energy. "Sometimes you are so busy you don't have time to think of esoteric things like what drives you. I love what

I do. That drives me. And I've just always been real approval-oriented, wanting to please my parents, teachers, friends. That's been a real asset in my life . . . and a real liability. But I've learned it's not important to please everybody. It's very different for me now."

She can't help it if she's naturally ebullient and unable to take it easy. "I can't just do one thing. I'm no different than I was as a child dressing up Zorro my dog and putting on a three-ring circus in the backyard. The only difference is that I put on a national ten-ring circus now."

Her business calendar is always full. For instance, in January 1995 she was scheduled to be in a concert with Philbin, sing the national anthem at the Super Bowl, and do two concerts in Las Vegas with Philbin. In spring, her new CD of lullabies for children would hit the compact disc bins. Too, *Listen to My Heart: Lessons in Love, Laughter and Lunacy,* her book about her wacky conversations with Cody, would soon grace the bookstores. And of course she would cohost *Live With Regis And Kathie Lee* every weekday.

She is so strait-laced that she never feuds with anyone, despite what the tabloids say. "The tabloids would have us believe that every week I'm feuding with Vanna White and Delta Burke or Della Reese; it doesn't really seem to matter. I don't even feud with my ex-husband. That's not part of what I'm all about at all. And I'm not feuding with Regis, ever. And I'm not feuding with Frank over a baby. We have an understanding about that. I don't like conflict. It's very difficult for me."

That may well be so, but she will not pretend to like immoral people in order to avoid a conflict. She is adamant about her feelings that the heavy metal band Metallica is "Satanic." Also, at the Grammy awards during a standing ovation for James Brown, an ex-con, she refused to rise.

In 1993 she threatened to quit *Live With Regis and Kathie Lee* because she didn't like one of the guests who was booked for the show. That guest represented everything that she hated, everything that conflicted with her Moral Majority image.

The guest was Mark DeCarlo, host of the dating-game–style TV show *Studs*. When Kathie Lee voiced her objections to the producers of her show about booking DeCarlo, they ignored her and went ahead and invited him anyway. He appeared on a show during Christmas week, no less.

"That's when I almost quit," Kathie Lee said.

She was incensed over the fact that the producers had paid no attention to her objections. "Why [do] we promote promiscuity when people are dying from unsafe sex? Why give this guy five minutes of airtime when what he does, to me, is offensive?"

On the syndicated show *Studs* a pair of men and three women crow over their sexual exploits as the audience cheers them on. Kathie Lee didn't think such a show should be promoted on *Live With Regis and Kathie Lee* in the Age of AIDS.

She related her tête-a-tête with her producers in the following manner:

"I got very angry. I said, 'If he comes on, I'm going to ask him how he can do such a thing in a time when sexual promiscuity is killing people.' I had to ask him that and, of course, some people came up to me and said, 'How could you be so rude?'"

Philbin bore out her decision. "She, of course, is Joan of Arc. I'm just a regular person. But I agree with her on that. Sure, we have certain standards on our show, and I think we should adhere to them."

Kathie Lee marvels at how busy she is nowadays. "I'm getting more opportunities now in a month than I used to get in a year—try ten years—things I would have loved to have done five years ago. It's so much more than I ever dreamed it would be. . . . You'd think: Is she never satisfied? But I get bored easily, and I have to keep doing different things—growing."

In other words, she may quit *Live With Regis and Kathie Lee* soon. "After nine years, as wonderful as it's been, and as much as I adore Regis—and he and I will be friends forever—I feel like the old Peggy Lee song, 'Is That All There Is?'"

Philbin couldn't agree more. "That's kind of like how I feel about the show. I've done it for eleven years, nine with Kathie, and it's been terrific, but there's a sameness year after year after year. We'll have to say goodbye someday, and that's going to be a sad day for the two of us because it's been terrific."

It's not that Kathie Lee doesn't want to keep working. She loves to work, and has often attested to that fact—in words as well as in deeds. But at the same time, she doesn't want to be typed as simply a singer, or, perhaps, as simply a talk-show host. She feels that she must grow as a person, as an artist, and as a musician, as she has said before.

Kathie Lee has managed to cut down a bit on a few of her many assignments. She has cut back on her commercials for Carnival Cruises. She has a contract with Revlon, which she has minimized to an extent. She does work for the Home Furnishings Council. And, of course, there is her new line of clothing. But essentially, that's another story, which will be covered in detail later on.

She once mused to an interviewer that she might someday, with all her interests and involvements, find that all she could manage to squeeze out would be five days a week with *Live With Regis and Kathie Lee*. If so, Kathie Lee feels—so be it.

The trouble is, Kathie Lee has great difficulty saying no to anyone: "That's the hardest part. It wasn't like that for a long time in my life. I used to peddle everything to everybody."

Whenever she sings at a concert Kathie Lee tosses and turns in her bed the night before, so obsessed is she with her career. At a recent concert in New Orleans, one of the many she performs every year, she spent a bad and sleepless night on the eve of her performance.

Kathie Lee lay awake the night before, worrying. What if no one comes? "I said over and over that no one would come. Then, in the car, we turned the corner and there they were. They were lined up with their babies down the street, and I started crying, 'Oh, my God. They came! They came!' I felt like Sally Field when she gave that acceptance speech at the Academy Awards: 'You like me, you really like me.' Everyone made fun of her. But I know just how she felt."

Regarding her singing career, Kathie Lee becomes annoyed with people who refuse to accept her as a singer as well as a talk-show host. "I can't be all things to all people. The hard part is that people see me as a talk-show host. But this is not a hobby. I've done this professionally."

A dedicated performer, she's always nervous before a concert because: "I really want it to be good. I did Freddy's five years ago and got lousy reviews, but I sold out and got standing ovations. Why? I don't know and I won't waste time thinking about it. The people paid and had a good time and that makes it a success. I've succeeded in this business so long because I know what I'm not. Critics don't buy tickets. If I please the people who buy tickets, then I'm a success."

In a profile on Kathie Lee in *New York Woman* in 1989, Leah Rozen gave her high marks for combining her own special talent and sophistication with what Rozen called a "perkiness bordering on carbonation." And she went on to describe Kathie Lee as "the perfect TV cutie, except she's wicked."

In fact, Rozen went on to say, "That's her charm, and it's why so many of us are fans of hers, albeit covertly. It will never be hip to like her—Linda Ellerbee she ain't—but then again she's not delivering the news."

Her most outstanding attribute, Rozen wrote, is the fact that she has "no verbal filter." She simply says what first pops into her active mind. And it's usually funny; if not side-splitting, it's perceptive. Rozen then selected several "great moments" of Kathie Lee as follows:

She recalled Kathie Lee's conversation with Esther Williams, the swimmer-actress who made a number of aquatic films in the forties and fifties: "How did you keep yourself from getting pruney?"

She mentioned the times she pointed out that her cohost, Regis Philbin, had hair growing out of his ears.

Alex Witchel wrote in the *New York Times* in 1991 that the formula for *Live With Regis and Kathie Lee* was a simple one. "He's the backbone, she's the butterfly. Like a skilled hostess circa 1954, it is her job to look glamorous, keep the conversation light, and counter her often cantankerous cohost with her own cute-as-a-button brand of openness."

He went on. "She'll say anything in the interest of being unpretentious, like the time she caught her gardener urinating in the backyard or recounting the most intimate details of her breast feeding."

According to Witchel, Kathie Lee admitted: "I make fun of myself for a living every day of my life. You can either laugh with us or at us."

As has been recorded already, the Nielsen ratings by the beginning of the 1991–92 season showed *Live With Regis and Kathie Lee* to be the fastest rising national talk show on television.

"Kathie Lee's seven-year pairing with cohost Regis Philbin has transformed the two talk-show hosts into hot national celebrities with ratings to die for," Joanna Powell wrote in *Redbook* in 1992. "Their loopy free-for-all keeps more than three and a half million television sets tuned in."

In fact in the fall of 1992 the syndication statistics of *Live* passed the two-hundred-station mark. At the beginning of the 1993–94 season, the show had a national daytime rating of 4.5, right up there with *Donahue* and just behind *Sally Jessy Raphael*. Sometimes, in fact, it was number one in its time slot in cities where it was not in competition with Oprah Winfrey.

All of Kathie Lee's reviews are not ecstatic, though. In August 1994, she performed a benefit concert at Avery Fisher Hall in New York City. The *New York Times* covered the concert, with Stephen Holden writing, "A deeply conventional lounge singer whose tastes lean toward Broadway standards, she repeatedly reaches for the emotive grandeur of Barbra Streisand but comes out sounding more like Helen Reddy with a touch of Liza Minelli."

New York magazine covered her too, in a more kindly, gentle fashion. "Do not panic," its reviewer wrote. "Her voice is a sweet, clear one, the kind that wins heartland talent shows by the thousands."

Maybe her joke to a *Hartford Courant* reporter best exemplifies her own self-deprecating image. As a reporter shook hands with her in 1992, Kathie Lee said, "Sorry, I was in the ladies room. At least it's clean."

Like Kathie Lee.

Regis and Kathie Lee as Entertainers:

Close-up on Live

O n their show, Regis and Kathie Lee talk about important things, such as Kathie Lee's seeing David Letterman pick his nose while sitting in his car in a traffic jam. Or perhaps Kathie Lee's revelation that her husband, Frank, the famous football commentator, had sleepwalked in the raw and fetched up in bed with the nanny. "Boy! I heard about it from everybody," groaned golden-boy Gifford after the nationally telecast program.

These gossipy tidbits all take place during the first fifteen to twenty minutes of *Live With Regis and Kathie Lee*. Philbin calls it the "host chat" section, during which Kathie Lee likes to talk about her young son Cody and Philbin likes to talk about Notre Dame football and his pet peeve for the day.

It is not only Kathie Lee who is into disclosing the most intimate details of her life. Philbin too has a penchant for chatting about exciting details of his life like, for example, his 1990 kidney-stone operation. He even went so far as to bring one of the stones onto the set for an early morning show-and-tell.

Philbin brings up familial details, too. He calls his mother-in-law Ethel Senese "Hello! Let's Eat!" when talking about her on the show. The nickname has stuck. Even the clerks at Bloomingdale's call her that when she buys clothes there.

Philbin's wife, Joy, is incensed but she is realistic concerning her family's fame. "I realize there is nothing I can do about it, but there have been times that I have literally screamed at the TV."

Philbin believes the host chat segment is successful because "in the opening, we never lie about anything. Always truth and honesty. It's all the truth, so that makes it funny."

Host chat is unscripted and unrehearsed. The two hosts don't even see each other before the show airs. Doing an hour of work with her is all Philbin can take of Kathie Lee "Do you know what it's like everyday with *that buzz saw*! It's *not easy*!"

Live With Regis and Kathie Lee has turned out to be a show for the entire family. Kathie Lee frequently gets letters that say, "Thank you for a show that I can actually sit and watch with my family and not be embarrassed by."

As mentioned before, Philbin is tired of all the sex topics on the other talk shows. "You know, the sex stuff, it's really a scream isn't it? 'Donahue: Couple arrested after having sex! Jenny Jones: Making money with your body! Geraldo: Women in relationships with serial killers!' Ha ha ha ha ha! That's not us, you know. We have on Tempest Bledsoe and *think we're getting crazy*!"

Of course Philbin's main obsession is to take an active part in checking out the Nielsen ratings to make sure he is still on top of a bandwagon that is moving. In most cases it is Michael Gelman, his producer-director, who brings him the good or bad news. But not always. Philbin has been known to break into the middle of a show and announce triumphantly that *Live* is outscoring all the opposition.

Depending on his mood—which is unpredictable, naturally—Philbin may stop anyone in the hall to discuss one-sidedly the superiority of the Nielsens that morning. David Bianculli, one of New York's top-rated television columnists, found himself the focus of a Regis Philbin ratings diatribe one morning and wrote a column about it.

The telephone conversation with Bianculli occurred because of the upcoming "1994 Miss America Pageant" in Atlantic City, to be emceed by Regis and Kathie Lee. It was simply a matter of Philbin's chatting with Bianculli about the pageant. The two discussed how Regis and Kathie Lee planned to approach the event.

Yes, Philbin agreed. He would be acting just a little more reverent at Atlantic City than on his own show. He felt that the Pageant people deserved that. Then, dispensing with that subject, he began chatting about ongoing and intense contract talks for *Live* at ABC-TV.

Suddenly Regis was the Regis everyone else knows on national television. He began to do his put-upon role. He thought the stage set they were forced to work in was just awful. He said it was tired, weary, burnt out, and badly needed some kind of updating.

"I go over to the Letterman show," he told Bianculli. And Bianculli burst out laughing. His laughter more than his words underlined his feeling for the absurd contrast in the two different performers, as well as the two different sets.

"Why not?" Regis snapped, offended. "Look at my ratings as opposed to David's! I'm right there with him. I'm looking at yesterday's overnights [New York TV ratings]. Are you ready, Bianculli?"

Bianculli was ready.

"Look at this. A twenty-six share. *Oprah*, twenty-two share. . . . How dare Bianculli laugh when I say I need an updated studio? Let's just see who's got a higher share than me. Nothing on CBS. Nothing on NBC. I'm looking at daytime, nighttime, prime time— *Wheel of Fortune* ties me. Oh, look, I lose it to *All American Girl*, with a thirty share. The only thing to beat me in New York.

"We're a runaway beer truck! We're out of control! *Marilu Henner*, six share. *Jane Whitney*, twelve share. *Gordon Elliott*, thirteen share. *Stomping! Moving! Crushing!*"

70

A pause.

"What was your question again?"

Well, not exactly a Regis-Kathie Lee exchange, but not bad, considering—and it points out Philbin's continued obsession with ratings.

During host chat the two cohosts always ask a trivia question, which is supposed to be answered by a viewer over the phone. If the answer is correct, Philbin sticks a pin in a map on the wall to indicate where the viewer lives. Also during this segment, Philbin holds up newspapers and comments on their headlines—which is similar to a routine Jay Leno does, except that Leno uses writers, whereas Philbin ad libs on the spot.

After host chat there is a celebrity guest who walks onto the stage and is interviewed by Philbin and Kathie Lee as they sit among their sparse furnishings.

When contretemps occur—and they frequently do—Philbin uses them as grist for his comedic mill. Take the time actor Craig T. Nelson, from *Coach*, walked onto the show.

Philbin: "I think it was his first talk show. He wound up looking at a doorway, with his back to the audience and his back to me. So, I turned my back to him, and we did the interview back to back."

However, he admits: "Most everybody is a terrific guest once they relax and open up."

Philbin has made hay of other blunders on the show too.

"The other day we did a romance novel cover," he told *All Talk* in December 1994. "During the commercial break, I was trying to get out of the costume and into my clothes. The camera came back up, and I was zipping up my fly. I said, 'Yes! I have a fly and I have to zip it up!' I zipped it up. You have to go with what's happening at the moment."

To add to the spontaneity of the show, Philbin and Kathie Lee don't even walk onto the stage together. They make separate entrances, eyeing each other as they do so to find out the going mood of the day.

71

As of 1994 they were the third most popular talk-show personalities in the United States, according to a Lou Harris poll. Only Oprah Winfrey, number one, and David Letterman, number two, beat them out.

The chemistry between Philbin and Kathie Lee is so good because, as she puts it, "I'm as comfortable with him as anyone I've ever known in my life." The secret is a simple one. "It's so simple that it's deceptive. Nobody really understands. We just have great fun together!"

Philbin feels Kathie Lee is the best cohost he has ever worked with, better even than *Entertainment Tonight's* spunky, bright-eyed Mary Hart, with whom he did a stint some years ago. Kathie Lee is better, he believes, because, along with a sometimes wicked tongue, she is a totally spontaneous, no-nonsense person.

Philbin, of course, is spontaneous too, which can, on occasion, land him in hot water. On one episode he couldn't help but comment about a nun's spectacles. Oversized, wraparound goggles that all but covered her entire face, they inspired Philbin to ask, "Where'd you get those glasses, Sister, Mario Andretti?"

The tabloids had a Roman holiday once they got hold of this remark. They labeled him "outrageous" and "tart-tongued." What kind of a remark was that for a nice devout Catholic like Philbin to make?

Philbin insisted that, taken "in context," it was a comment meant in fun. All Kathie Lee could say about the incident was "Outregis!"

Philbin has a habit—perhaps an intentional one—of getting guests' names mixed up. When Dweezil Zappa visited the show, Philbin introduced him as Dreezil. Dweezil got back at him by calling him Remus. This is all part of the cobbled-together style of the show, as if the whole shebang was conceived seconds before it hit the airwaves. Or, perhaps, after.

Sometimes the show has a public service aspect to it. For example, Kathie Lee and Philbin have had precancerous moles excised from their skins on air by a dermatologist. Watching the operation, thousands of viewers decided to undergo the same treatment.

Kathie Lee is not afraid to act human on the show. "When my bra strap's showing, I make a thing about it. When my slip's up to here, I pull it down. For a long time there's been an antiseptic look to television. A lot of perfect people. Regis and I celebrate our humanity, in a sense. We are imperfect people in an imperfect world."

In describing the chitchatting duo, she has this to say: "We're the two most uncool people in America. I love my husband. I believe in God. I adore my [children]. We live in the country. Reege is a Catholic father of four and loves his wife. We never try to be hip."

She has said elsewhere, "I'm really a very kind person and I'm a good person. I'm not perfect, but I never ever set out to hurt anybody. Ever."

Her Little Goody Two-Shoes, upbeat persona counteracts Philbin's curmudgeonly one in a positive fashion. Philbin has his own take on why he and she work so well together:

"It comes from the fact that Kathie Lee and I both have backgrounds in live performing. We like being informal. We like being spontaneous. We like to say whatever—or, almost whatever—comes into our heads. Whatever it is we're doing, I wouldn't change a thing. After all these years in television, I think I finally got it right."

The two discuss only rinky-dink topics, nothing abstruse.

As Tom Shales of the *Washington Post* saw it, it's the chemistry between Philbin and Kathie Lee that makes earwax, ingrown hairs, pimples, and warts funny — and "chemistry is the most important element on television. You can't force it, and when it happens, it's wonderful."

On a typical morning, Regis was griping to the world about the new country house where he had just moved, the boiler that didn't work in it, and the contractor who was on hire to fix the boiler but never showed up.

Then Regis went on complaining about having to rent a car to drive to Manhattan to purchase accoutrements for the jinxed house, and, naturally, he couldn't find a parking space to save his life. At the end of his tirade, he withdrew something from his pocket. Two somethings. Parking tickets.

Philbin held up the two tickets and said, "I'm the only guy to get two parking tickets in two different places in two and a half minutes." Pause. "And I don't even own a car!" Pause. "Boy, am I *aggravated*!"

The 150 people in the studio audience, the majority of them women, cheered.

Actually, the secret of the successful bickering between Regis and Kathie Lee is this: the more trivial the subject the bigger the laugh. Of course, it all depends on a sense of humor to bring off the griping. It's a thing that both of the cohosts have in abundance.

Topics of humor range all the way from hangnails to split ends. Kathie Lee put it this way in May 1988: "Our show is fun because Regis and I have fun together. Most of all, we love to make fun of each other. If I have a zit on my nose, people know that Regis and I have the kind of relationship where he's going to bring it up."

Michael Gelman's hat is off to Philbin and Kathie Lee. The executive producer told *TV Guide* in February 1992, "The audience loves to watch them walk a tightrope. They couldn't take as many chances if they didn't care about each other. Though they're married to other people, there is some kind of dynamic between them, but what makes the great chemistry is the fact that viewers have developed a relationship with them. They're in on the chemistry."

"Yet," said Philbin at the same interview, "there is that extra something that people get out of our openness. Nobody else does it like that. We understand each other's inner feelings."

"Reege is a sex symbol to the menopause set," Kathie Lee chipped in.

"C'mon! Where's Kathie Lee going to go without me?"

In essence the show is about nothing. It's not what they say, it's how they say it that cracks people up.

Regarding the host chat segment of the show, David Letterman once said, full of respect for a fellow comedian, "Time that opening segment. That thing sometimes goes eighteen, twenty minutes—and it's *nothing*."

"It's hard to describe what this show is about," Philbin agrees. "It's about two people in a relationship, and the things that spin off that."

He goes on. "It's deceptive what we do. It's twenty minutes, and it's all ad lib. I don't know anybody else who dares to go on television without knowing what . . . they're going to talk about."

Despite the show's success, Gelman thinks Kathie Lee talks too much about her cute kids.

She is quick to defend herself. "Gelman and I have so little in common that there's always a battle, it seems, in terms of values, in terms of taste. We just rarely agree on anything."

"He tries to tell me what our audience wants, and I laugh. I go: 'How do you know? You're single. You're male. You've just turned thirty. You live in New York City. Don't tell me what a mother in Iowa with four children, who stays at home, wants to hear about!'"

She continues, her hackles up. "Regis is Mr. Out about Town. I'm a full-time mother. I go home, and it's rare that my husband and I go out. Our lives revolve around our children. So, what else do I have to talk about on the air every morning?"

Philbin refuses to eat out with her; he did it once, and it simply sank the show the following day. "The other night we went out together, we had dinner, and the next morning it was so strange because we had *already* shared something together and there wasn't much to talk about."

Gelman is one of the very few people in the world today—like Madonna and Cher—who needs only one name. Once it's uttered, everyone *knows* who Gelman is, and what he's supposed to be doing.

According to Tanya Barrientos in the *Chicago Tribune*, Gelman is "probably the best-known television producer since Fred DeCordova, the guy Johnny Carson used to tease."

And there is a definite similarity. DeCordova was Carson's producer-director, too. As is Gelman producer-director of *Live With Regis and Kathie Lee*.

In a way, Gelman serves as a punching bag for chief puncher Regis Philbin on *Live*. A typical exchange is the following quite recent one:

"I've been making football picks for years," Philbin says, with that trademark crescendo in his voice just beginning to make the words ring out. Now, at the peak of speech, he goes on, disdainfully. "You'd think Gelman would make a chart, play some football music. No! He just stands there while the show is produced for him."

A double put-down done by the double put-down master. Gelman not only doesn't make a chart to show Regis's picks, but he lets the show be produced without lifting a finger—and he's the producer!

Kathie Lee is not far behind Regis in her ability to taunt Gelman. She was angry one morning about the lighting on the set. It seemed faint. Nobody could see them clearly. And she came on strong.

"Did Gelman fix the lighting? Noooo, that would cost money."

But that's mild stuff compared to what happened in May 1994. The first thing Kathie Lee heard about it was that *Live* would be broadcasting a clip from the hit cop show *NYPD Blue*—without bothering to bleep out the naughty words. It was the naughty words and the nudity that were bothering Kathie Lee.

She went almost ballistic. She glared at Gelman and briefly and grimly apologized in advance to her listeners for what they would see later on the show. Regis was caught off-guard. He giggled something awkwardly, trying to laugh it all off as just one of those silly feud things.

In the event, the guest star from the acclaimed ABC-TV cop show, actor James McDaniel, who plays Lieutenant Arthur Fancy, dug in his heels and refused to go on the air. Gelman wound up with a cancellation—and empty time to fill.

Regis and Kathie Lee filled it all right, but things were getting just a little bit hairy on-camera as well as off. The feud didn't end there.

Some time later, Regis had what he called a great idea for a *Live* spin-off. In a typically Philbinesque manner, he turned to Kathie Lee and Gelman and said, "You two kids, who have had such a wonderful relationship lately, could have one show and Regis could maybe have *his own*!" Accompanied by a manic grin.

Tension built backstage. The feud continued to widen the gap between Kathie Lee and Gelman. But Gelman wouldn't admit there was a problem. He took it in stride as something to give the show a bit of an edge.

"I love babies, I love James McDaniel, I love Regis and Kathie Lee, I love my ponytail, and I just want everybody to be happy."

After that Regis and Kathie Lee spent a great deal of time inventing ways to aggravate Gelman. One of the things they made him do was stick his finger in the blades of a fan.

Then they had him shot out of a huge cannon—Gelman becoming a human ballistic missile, soaring down Columbus Avenue. Then they replayed that crowning insult in slow motion, laughing at his form as he came whishing out of the cannon's mouth.

Things eventually simmered down. "We had some strongly worded discussions," Kathie Lee admitted to the *Ladies Home Journal* in September 1994. Kathie Lee's problem was that they were copycatting other talk shows. "Why should we be like every other show? I didn't feel they [Regis and Gelman] had a better grasp of our audience than I did. I said I was going to leave if things didn't change."

Things obviously did change.

Kathie Lee and Michael Gelman finally have what she called "an understanding and respect we didn't have there for a while."

But the "feud" did put a crimp in the 1994 contract talks. The new contracts are concurrent; that is, she and Regis will be negotiating at the same time together. The idea is simple: if Regis goes, Kathie goes, too.

"I don't want to be stuck doing the show with anybody else," Kathie Lee says.

And nothing ever changes. Gelman always stands in the shadows of the ABC-TV studio, his arms behind his back, watching, listening, studying. He has a big role when the camera turns on him, usually in the case of Regis's desiring a little punching-bag time.

He nods. He smiles. Sometimes he talks.

This young man is thirty-three years old and is a fresh-faced New Yorker. He wears his chin-length hair pulled back in a professionally chic ponytail. He seemed to come with the job. But the seeming here is not the reality. He started out as a free-lance producer-director and gradually was assimilated into the staff.

Quite soon he was the only one at the top.

But how did he manage it when Regis and Kathie Lee both had constant words to say about his work?

Well, it's a role he, Regis, and even Kathie Lee play. Being Regis and Kathie Lee's fall guy is not Gelman's main job at all. The show that Regis has said many times goes on in spite of Gelman. That's a gag.

Gelman phrases it a bit differently. "That's an old shtick of his," Gelman says about Philbin's on-air bitching. "He liked the way I reacted to it, that it made me a little uncomfortable and that I wouldn't try to throw out one-liners and try to be funny."

So Gelman the goat has been doing his thing ever since—and he's become an important part of the show. In fact, he has become famous, if that's the proper word. He has fans all over the place. They stand and wait for him to deliver his autograph to them. People want to have their picture taken with him.

Gelman: "That's not who I am."

Offstage in a cornflower blue T-shirt under a black suit, wearing Doc Martens on his feet, Gelman broods somewhat about his persona and how Regis and Kathie Lee have made him something he really isn't.

"Sometimes I don't come off as the strong person I think I am." He smiles faintly. "People don't realize it, but that's less than one percent of my job." He means playing for Regis and Kathie Lee.

The truth of the matter is—and neither Regis nor Kathie Lee would ever quibble about it—that Gelman is actually the backbone of the syndicated *Live* show, which continues to enjoy those high ratings. He has had, in fact, three Emmy nominations, although he never came up with the brass ring.

"The more important part of my job," he told the *Chicago Tribune*, "is deciding who comes on the show, how we spend our money, and what we're going to do."

All his life, Gelman has dreamed about being in show business. He wanted to be behind the scenes, pulling the strings that make the thing go.

"I never wanted to be one of the pretty faces in front of the camera," he says with a rueful smile. "Although, now that it's happened, I have to admit I'm enjoying the attention."

The one secret word in Gelman's vocabulary is usually never mentioned casually. He wants "control" of the show and the way it twists and turns.

Other than that, there's nothing that he doesn't already have that he wants, except maybe a family. Is he eligible?

He says, "I'm single and I've got a job, if that's eligible."

As for Regis Philbin, he much prefers the chemistry—or whatever it is—between him and Kathie Lee to that between him and Joey Bishop on Bishop's show.

On *Live With Regis and Kathie Lee* Philbin is the king. The role of second fiddle never sat well with him. He knew he had what it takes to star in his own talk show and his legions of fans are living proof of that.

He doesn't like the other talk shows. "They all copycat themselves. They get people on who are willing to expose themselves, all their past sins, and everything else.

"I hate it. That's not my style. They certainly have people watching them. But I think they've perverted the taste of America."

Philbin feels the other talk shows, by being repugnant, help make his thrive. "I think the reason we are successful is simply because we are different."

He feels more secure now with his style of humor. "I had dry periods where I was scared, out of work, thinking, 'What the heck am I going to do?' I felt my brand of television was so intimate that critics missed it entirely."

The critics may have missed it entirely, but the viewers did not. On the show one morning a butcher appeared. It was his job to demonstrate to Regis and Kathie Lee how to do pork cuts—and at the same time, explain it to the audience.

Regis was puzzled. He looked at one of the pork cuts and frowned. Regis, in no way appearing embarrassed that he did not know the answer, immediately asked, What *were* these strange things? And where did they come from?

Kathie Lee glanced at him to see if he was teasing. He wasn't. "A pig, Reege," she said solemnly.

Regis Philbin, it developed, was not putting on an act of any kind. His wife, Joy, has often said that he is just like that at home the minute he's off the air. She attributes it to the fact that he's just a bit forgetful. There is always a problem of names, with Regis. As any viewer knows, he frequently mixes up names in his head—names of some of the most known celebrities.

But the family puts up with him. His mother-in-law frequently telephones, and if Regis answers the phone, she will dutifully say: "Hi, Reege. This is Ethel. You know. *Ethel*, your mother-in-law."

A great day dawned recently. Regis came on the show walking at least six inches off the floor. He had recently learned how to make coffee. Joy had showed him how to do it. He had memorized it: "Three scoops in. Six cups of water. Turn the switch. I make coffee!"

But sometimes gloom descends over Regis Philbin. He hates being thought of as a guy who's unable to do anything. Who wants to be known as an expert at doing nothing? He had always wanted to play the piano. And sing. And do the million and one things other entertainers do. But he had never succeeded.

Although once he made an album for Mercury Records. Once. And once only. Period.

Kathie Lee has attributed the success of their partnership to having "a completely different type of program. We call ourselves alternative programming. We're not doom and gloom. We're really a variety show. We're up and happy and funny."

It hasn't always been easy, she concedes. "We've had pretty formidable competition in the past. When we first started in New York, for fourteen years Phil Donahue had been absolute king of the nine A.M. time slot. Nobody was ever able to make a dent against him. But he moved to four o'clock in the afternoon as soon as we became number one. Now, he battles Winfrey in the afternoon."

Philbin can't believe he is at the top of his game after all his years of struggle. He feels he is the same person he always was. Even his wakeup regimen hasn't changed.

"I get up at seven-thirty, take a tablespoon of cod-liver oil and two tablespoons of milk for my arthritis. I take my shower, shave, have some breakfast, go back and brush my teeth."

He's often said that it is the ability to survive and endure that makes a show biz personality a success. It is that very quality of "durability" that he admires so much in the Miss America contestants.

"Having been around the contest the last couple years [as a cohost], I've admired the 'stick-to-itiveness' of some of the contestants. They keep coming back. They won't take no for an answer. Some hang in there for years. Perseverance can pay off."

Although he does admit that the sixty-year-old brunette from Alabama probably won't win no matter how many times she keeps coming back.

* * *

Philbin arrives at the *Live With Regis and Kathie Lee* studio each day at 8:30 A.M. and talks to none of the guests before the show. "It's a great schedule. Doing the show without a script eliminates a lot of work."

Located at the ABC-TV studio on the corner of Columbus Avenue and Sixty-Seventh Street in New York, the set can hold two hundred-odd fans, who watch as the show is taped.

It is Michael Gelman's job to warm up the audience before Regis and Kathie Lee make their appearance. But Gelman is no comic in residence. He merely explains what is going to happen and tells the audience that they are expected to react exactly as they feel like responding.

He also assures them that it is all right to cheer anything they think is good and to laugh heartily at anything they think is funny. And if it isn't any good, to be sure to keep it to themselves.

Although it's called a warm-up, it's really a kind of a cool-down. But it always seems to work—particularly in the laid-back milieu of *Live With Regis and Kathie Lee*.

When Philbin makes his entrance, the audience waves at him and some of them try to ask him questions. Then Kathie Lee enters and host chat begins.

According to Gelman, "Morning TV gets less respect than it deserves. The money it generates is more [of] an equal to late-night. The HUT [Homes Using Television] levels are about the same. We should be compared to *Arsenio Hall* or *David Letterman*, but morning gets no respect. We are trying to change that perception."

There's another reason the show should be earning more respect—the quality of its guests. Said Gelman, "We're getting a lot of 'A' names now like Madonna or Liza Minnelli. Celebrities are asking to come on because they know they will be presented in a good light."

The show's family reputation works in its favor in upgrading the celebrity guest list. The program has a small production staff of eight members. They try to help set the homey tone, which is best exemplified in the host chat segment.

Gelman prefers this "friendly and personal approach," especially during sweeps weeks when stations are at each other's throats trying to get the highest possible Nielsen ratings.

"As issue talk shows multiply," Gelman continues, "it gets harder to say something new. Sweeps is a joke. So we've gotten away from topical stuff and go even farther away to counterprogram. Our show is on a trend hitting the country, the more warm family of the 1990s."

As of 1991 the Nielsen Cassandra rankings gave *Live With Regis and Kathie Lee* a 3.7 rating among women. It was the fourth highest rated talk show and ranked twentieth among all syndicated shows with respect to female viewers. It came in twenty-fifth among all syndicated shows in the twenty-five to fifty-four-year-old group and in the fifty and older group. It was thirty-first in the group of women aged eighteen to forty-nine and thirty-eighth among eighteen to thirty-four-year-old women.

Mort Marcus, the senior vice president of sales for Buena Vista Television, the syndicator of *Live With Regis and Kathie Lee*, said of the show in 1991:

"We'd love for it to be on in early fringe instead of morning, but it has to be the right time period and the right station. We've found if a station leaves it in a time period, it grows. The show has long-term value and will stay on the air as long as those two [Philbin and Kathie Lee] want to do it."

Riding the wave of his success, Philbin plans to cash in on it by writing a book about his life for Hyperion, which has agreed to put up a million dollars for it. If Kathie Lee could write a bestseller, *I Can't Believe I Said That!*, then why not Philbin?

7

Regis as Husband:
The Family Philbin

Regis Philbin and his wife, Joy, live in a luxurious ten-room apartment on Manhattan's East Side. They have two daughters, Joanna, twenty, and Jennifer, nineteen.

When he is not shooting his show or doing one of the twenty-five-odd nightclub acts he does each year with Kathie Lee, he may be found in his home office off the master bedroom. The office is filled with a massive wooden desk, a Louis Quinze chair, family pictures, memorabilia, books, and a TV. There is also a floor-to-ceiling curtain over the window.

The Philbins bought the apartment in 1984. They have decorated it twice already. In fact, the first time they renovated they taped it for *Live With Regis and Kathie Lee*.

Philbin is proud of the results. The rest of the apartment, like his home office, is modestly decorated. His studio office at ABC on Manhattan's West Side is equally modest. It's chockablock with blowups of himself and Kathie Lee Gifford, a Knute Rockne poster, a photo of an Oleg Cassini ad featuring a youthful Philbin, and an autographed picture of the Hollywood actor Van Johnson. If you look closely enough you can see Johnson's inscription on the glossy: "God Bless You, From Your Biggest Fan, Van."

The office also contains a lamp that has a football helmet for a base. Tallying with the sports motif are autographed basketballs and baseball caps. A colossal toy albino tiger, given to him as a gift by Siegfried and Roy, takes up a large part of the room.

On the sofa lies a throw pillow with one of Philbin's favorite quotes embroidered on it:

> "Never try to teach a pig to sing. It wastes your time and annoys the pig."   —MARK TWAIN

Meanwhile, back at the ranch, so to speak, Philbin's apartment contains a living room designed for amiable socializing. The relaxing earth tones, flowers, comfortable couches, soft thick carpets, and dim lighting convey a mood of conviviality.

"We've tried to make it as warm as possible," Philbin told *McCall's* in March 1994.

He has the furniture arranged in a tight circle in the den section of the living room, providing guests with an opportunity for intimate conversations.

"On my show I don't like to be too far from my guests. When you're up close with somebody, you can lower your voice and they can hear you. It's warmer."

Yet the furniture placement does not make you feel trapped. Adequate space has been left for guests who want to depart.

Before entertaining guests, Philbin sets hors d'oeuvres on the coffee table for snacking. "People are nervous when they walk into a room," he says. "Being able to pick up something delicious to eat relaxes them."

Philbin's guest list includes such luminaries as Kathie Lee and Frank Gifford (though not often) and gossip queen Claudia Cohen. For them Philbin plays the soothing music of Frank Sinatra, Tony Bennett, or Shirley Bassey and displays fresh potpourris to complement the ambiance.

To encourage conversation, Philbin poses a question to one guest, then asks the same question of each succeeding guest "so that everybody gets a shot at following up with their opinion." Above all, Philbin wants everyone to get a fair shake when putting in his two cents' worth.

Philbin is very solicitous toward timid souls. "Some people are intimidated when they get into a social situation with people they don't know, so they won't get in there and mix it up conversationally. I concentrate on the people who have trouble participating and try to bolster their confidence."

In short, even at home, Philbin is always playing the part of an interviewer. It's the role he is most comfortable with.

Before the Philbin family lived in New York, they resided in Los Angeles. They had a rough time adjusting to the move east. The children especially were deeply affected. To remedy the problem Philbin invited a transitional psychologist onto his show to counsel Joanna and Jennifer.

The psychologist discovered that the problem centered on an albino rat, a pet the girls had to leave behind with a neighbor in L.A. Philbin himself flew to L.A. to recover the abandoned rodent.

It is interesting to note that Joy Philbin closely resembles Kathie Lee Gifford in facial details. Therefore it's no surprise that Joy frequently substitutes on the show in the absence of Kathie Lee.

Kathie Lee believes that Regis is less "naughty" when his wife Joy is on the show with him. She also admits that she herself is less so when her husband Frank is on the show with her. She lays it all to "different dynamics" that are working when she and Regis are on with people other than their spouses. There's just less threat of repercussions later on, she feels.

Joy also drops in on the show in the guise of a guest expert on cooking, one of her favorite hobbies. When she guests on the show, she can act a tad outrageous.

For example:

Once she announced that Regis had an awful snoring problem. To prove her point and demonstrate how deafening his snoring was, she tape-recorded it one night and played it back on the show.

The stunt really paid off. Hundreds of letters poured in from fans, each with a specific "cure" for snoring. Nevertheless, after trying dozens of them, Regis found to his sorrow that he was snoring just as loud as usual, with no improvement in sight.

But snoring is only one of his many faults. Regis is as honest with himself as he is with anyone else. He has always known that Joy is much stronger than he is when it comes to family and personal crises. He also has no compunction about letting her bear the brunt of such crises.

Regis has always struggled with another personal imperfection: impatience. He wants things to be right—and right *immediately*. The horrible fact is that as he gets older, he finds that his impatience increases and his patience declines rapidly. Secretly, of course, he knows that impatience is all part of his dramatic shtick—and without it, he simply would not be the Regis Philbin known to his *Live* audience.

In 1991 the Philbins purchased a pied-à-terre in Fairfield County, not far from the Giffords' mansion in Greenwich, Connecticut.

Joy explained why they bought the house. "The tennis court was our main incentive. Tennis is our favorite recreation during the summer months."

Even before they moved in the Philbins used to play tennis there, and they let the former owner know that they would like to buy the house if he wanted to sell it.

It is a brick French provincial–style manse tucked away among tennis court, swimming pool, and landscaped, well-manicured grounds.

The entire family, including Jennifer and Joanna, make their way to the house almost every weekend during the summer months in order to play doubles and take a swim in the pool. To relax, they eat a casual meal on the porch with their numerous friends. With any other free time they have, they gobble down a gigantic bowl of popcorn while watching TV, preferably a sporting event with Notre Dame participating in it.

According to Joy, "Our lives revolve around the Notre Dame football schedule."

When they first moved in, Joy decided to redecorate. "The former owner preferred a more formal arrangement, but this is a weekend house for us, so we wanted to keep it relaxed."

Her biggest challenge was the kitchen. She decided to have it redone in French provincial style. To make her dream come true, she hired designer Lyn Peterson to build special accessories like an overhead pot rack and a center island. Fruitwood cabinets line the walls. The floor is terra cotta and the countertop is tiled.

In addition, she had the kitchen designed to fit in with her personality. "I like to know what is going on while I am out in the kitchen, cooking. So we put in a pass-through between the kitchen and family room so that I can be a part of things [out there]."

The renovation of the kitchen meant decreasing the size of the adjacent porch by several feet. To compensate for the loss in area, the Philbins added two new skylights in the porch roof, enabling them to view the stars over their heads at night as they sit under the roof. The skylights, of course, help give the illusion that the porch is bigger than it really is.

Some interior design experts believe one cannot provide enough of a breath-taking view. With this in mind, the Philbins added a king-size bay window to the master bedroom, commanding a panoramic view of the lush greenery surrounding the house. The resulting impression is that of a very spacious bedroom. Joy had the bedroom painted pastel green and white so as not to compete with the natural colors of the vibrant scenery.

Joy has had plenty of experience in decorating houses. She and Philbin have owned seven homes during their twenty-four-year marriage. She did have advice designing this house, though, from the professional decorator Katherine Stephens, who helped her in choosing color coordination, fabrics, and the appropriate type of furniture.

This was the first time she hired an interior decorator to help furnish a dwelling. Before, Joy used to do "what so many people do—we walked into a furniture store without much idea of our taste. We ended up with a huge yellow sectional sofa and a coffee table with sharp corners. You can become very tired of a big yellow sofa. And I was always on the edge of my seat, worrying if our two girls would hit their heads on that glass coffee table."

This time around Joy was much more aware of what she wanted in a room as well as specific colors and textures she found most compatible with her taste.

"In this most recent house, I was more focused on what I like than when I started out. For example, I realized that we would be using the family room mainly in the winter, so I chose a red room. Previously, I did not have the courage to make a room red."

With her acquired knowledge of interior decorating, Joy soon landed a job as host of *Haven*, a weekly television series. The show, produced by the Home Furnishings Council, debuted in April 1994. *Haven* serves as a clearinghouse for home-furnishing trends. The council's purpose is to act as a bridge between furniture manufacturers, retailers, and consumers; *Haven* serves as the vehicle to showcase furniture and accessories makers' products.

Haven is not Joy's first series. When the Philbins lived in L.A., she used to be a cohost with her husband on *Health Styles*, a series broadcast on the Lifetime cable network. When she started raising her children she did not want a full-time television career and so she abandoned the show. Now, with her children grown up, she has plenty of time to resume her TV work.

As she once put it, "I enjoyed being a mother and raising those two little girls. I didn't want to miss that time. I get mail from women saying, 'Be prepared for the empty nest syndrome.' Because I have found another interest, I did not experience a sense of loss."

Asked who makes the decisions concerning interior decorating at the Philbin household, she answered, "I am the one making the selections, but I consult him. Regis was a little nervous when I talked about doing a canopy bed. He loves to watch TV in bed and he was afraid he wouldn't be able to see the screen."

When he has any spare time, Philbin likes to go to the movies or read. "All the newspapers, all the magazines, and books of the guests that I must interview."

Sometimes he will flick on the TV and eyeball the competition. He likes and respects Donahue, Raphael, Rivera, and Winfrey. What he doesn't respect are their topics of discussion.

He pointed out, "I'm sorry that they have all [excepting Winfrey, who has sworn off this type of programming] taken that tack, because in the long run it's going to hurt them. Only it's taking longer than I thought."

As for himself, he is quite happy, thank you. "I know what unhappiness is, and going back over the valleys of my professional and personal life I can appreciate where I am now, and it's a wonderful position to be in. Yeah, I've got a lot to be happy about."

The irascible Regis Philbin is just an act. If he is a "grinch," he's a happy and amusing grinch and not to be taken seriously when he grouses and grinches.

He has much to be happy about, including all his kids—by his first marriage and by his second. They never cease to amaze him.

Once, he recalled, "I helped [Joanna] put her baggage into [her boyfriend's] car and right across the street was the grammar school, P.S. 6, that both girls went to, and it hit me: 'Jeez, it's just a few years ago that I was holding their hands, taking them across the street to school and suddenly here's this vibrant young girl who's driving away with this guy.' You begin to look at your life in terms of theirs and as they go through these different milestones, you realize your time is up."

Philbin understands that his days are numbered. He likes to visit his daughter J.J. at Notre Dame, which she decided to attend in order to follow in her famous father's footsteps.

Philbin claims to be a friend of the Notre Dame football coach, Lou Holtz. He attends their games every time he gets the chance. His father inspired him to go to Notre Dame while young Regis was growing up. Though he graduated with a B.A. degree in sociology in 1953, Philbin called himself "a very, very average student."

He never became involved in sports there as a student, other than a bit of intramural boxing. His forte was playing the role of a prankster.

"I was always carrying on in the hallways. I used to twist this one kid's feet when he was asleep. I thought it was such a scream."

In December 1993, Philbin visited his old room, 222, in Zahm Hall. The three students living there weren't particularly impressed.

"Is it true that they made you be in your rooms by ten o'clock?" one of them asked him almost as if he were focusing on some important historical detail.

"I feel like the old elephant who has come home to die," answered Philbin with a somewhat hollow smile.

One of the other students said, "We have our own difficulties today. We have to have the girls home by twelve."

Philbin blinked a bit, his fatherly instincts aroused. "My daughter doesn't come over here, does she?"

The third student said, "She doesn't come to this floor, but I've seen her on the others."

Philbin huffed and puffed and did a put-upon Regis, his voice lowering ominously. "*Keep her out!*"

He then visited his daughter's room. Later he recalled, "It's a snake pit in there. I once opened up a closet full of dirty clothes, and I swear I heard somebody breathing."

There was a game on the floor titled "Party 'Til You Puke" lying among a bunch of clothes scattered about the room. "That's a health-department violation if ever I've seen one," Philbin groused.

Philbin's daughter, J.J., decided to attend Notre Dame because her father talked so much about the university during her younger years. She remembered that he was always boasting about the football coach Knute Rockne. Also, somebody called "the Gipper." Yet it was J.J.'s own decision to go to Notre Dame.

J.J. had always felt from her youngest years that she and her father were a lot alike. The two of them, she decided, had plenty of spirit. And that, of course, made them both ideal for the kind of school spirit rampant on the South Bend, Indiana campus.

Philbin knew his daughter was happy at his old alma mater, and that made him feel good—not only because it reinforced his own feelings about college life, but because he felt she had found herself there.

Later on that day, he and J.J. attended a Notre Dame-Boston College football game, which BC won.

As the gloom descended, Philbin quipped, "Imagine. I had this game today, and next week I've got Kathie Lee."

Philbin has been traveling a lot lately, and he's never found any place more compatible than the campus at South Bend. Not only does its beauty and peacefulness represent harmony to him, but he feels that Notre Dame brings one face-to-face with truth and justice.

Corny as it seems, he feels that the world would be a better place if everybody stuck to the golden rules of the South Bend school.

He once suggested to his good friend George Kelly, assistant to the Notre Dame director, that the two of them should buy a house next door to the campus when they retired. Then they could sit outside and see the golden dome of the college every morning. Also, Philbin told Kelly that when he died he wanted his ashes sprayed all over the campus.

8

Kathie Lee as Mother:
The Family Gifford

Kathie Lee and Frank Gifford have two children—Cody, age five and Cassidy Erin, age two. Kathie Lee can't get enough of her youngsters. She talks about them day and night to anyone and everyone.

For the record, Cody Newton Gifford was born amid great fanfare on March 22, 1990, in New York City at 1:28 A.M. The name "Cody" came from a football player friend of Frank Gifford's—Cody Risien—with the birth being announced by Regis Philbin on *Live With Regis and Kathie Lee* during the morning's taping.

Coincidentally, and unbeknownst to the Giffords at the time, was the fact that Cody Newton Gifford and Cody Risien shared not only the same first name, but the same birthday! As Cody Newton emerged into the world, Cody Risien turned thirty-three. Cody Newton was eight pounds, fifteen ounces, at birth.

On August 3, 1993, Cassidy Erin Gifford saw the first light of day at 8:17 A.M. in Greenwich Hospital, Greenwich, Connecticut, with father Frank Gifford in attendance. At 9:08 he telephoned Regis Philbin on the *Live* set and told him of the birth. Cassidy Erin weighed eight pounds, eleven ounces, at birth.

With the children and all, Kathie Lee has to agree that she has a perfect home life. "We have Frank's grandchildren [all five of them] wandering around, and Cody pee-peeing in the pool. It's like a little piece of paradise."

Like any good mother, she wants to make sure her children have as much fun growing up as she did when she was a child.

Referring to Cody in 1991, she said, "You have a very short time to be a child, and we're in such a rush to raise our children to be adults that they miss out on a childhood. And I want my son to have that as much as possible. I wasn't taught to read when I was one and given math tests when I was two. There's enough time in life for all that pressure.

"I know it's a competitive world, but a child who has love and a wonderful childhood will have a competitive edge over anybody who's been stuck in a room with a book. I want Cody to be a wonderful human being. The rest is just going to happen."

Chatting about Cody on TV, she came across as very human, thus attracting an even larger audience to her show.

"I guess having Cody made me more accessible to viewers. Instead of name-dropping about what glitzy event I went to the night before, I could talk about how Cody threw the pork chop at my sister and hit her left breast."

Kathie Lee has strong ideas about motherhood. She had thought that she would feel maternal love completely the very first time she held Cody, her firstborn, in her arms. She was surprised to find that what she felt more than love was simply protective-ness. Yet she need not have feared that love was lacking. Her love, she said, grew day by day, and watching her baby grow into a young son was a fascinating study in the evolution of life.

She was so startled at what was happening that she told her husband: "Can you believe we made this?"

Kathie Lee believes that every baby is an embodiment of hope. Each child starts out with the promise of a better life. And each child is born with the possibility that he or she can become one of mankind's leaders. Perhaps an artist, perhaps a scientist, perhaps a president. When two people come together for love, the child produced will hopefully embody the best of both of them.

She knows that both Cody and Cassidy will not grow up at all in the way both she and Frank Gifford grew up. Yet Cody and Cassidy are well on their way to a very comfortable life in the wealthy environs of Greenwich.

As she put it recently, "I make a lot of money. But I give away a lot of it, too. Every Christmas, Cody gives most of his toys away before he can get anything new."

Kathie Lee is not ashamed to admit she has lots of money. Despite her impressive income, she will not spoil her children, though she has no intention of rearing them in poverty, as Frank was.

She pointed out that her husband grew up during the Great Depression. The family was hard-working and struggled to succeed. She herself was a little luckier. "In my family we had a lot of love, but not a whole lot of money to spare. Cody's going to grow up knowing material things in a way that Frank and I didn't.

"So my biggest concern as a mother is how do I raise my child with the same values I was raised with—without the same circumstances? He's not going to know poverty, thank God, but how's he going to know that there are poverty-stricken people unless he sees them and learns to care about them?

"It's important that he never takes his life for granted and always has an attitude of gratitude."

Thanks to the Giffords' wealth, Kathie Lee cannot raise her children like most mothers. Along with her money come difficulties ordinary people will never know.

Contrary to what many people think, it's not easy to be rich. The Giffords decided when Cody was born that they could not raise him and any other children they might have the same way in which they were brought up.

It's easy enough for Kathie Lee to give Cody a quarter each

time he cleans his room. But after that, what? It would be impossible for Cody to get a paper route when he grew into his teens, because they were now worked by professionals. And the old-fashioned lemonade stand outside the house—as in Charles Shultz's comic strip *Peanuts*—is out of another century. Or seems to be.

Yet Kathie Lee has instigated a rather strict and stern discipline for Cody. She wants to be sure she doesn't crush his spirit, as could happen to someone under too tight a regimen. Kathie Lee's rules are strict, but not harsh. If Cody forgets to say "please," he doesn't get what he wants. And if he doesn't say "thank you," he can't keep what he has been given.

She has had her critics. Permissiveness took a great deal of edge off discipline in the nineteen-sixties. Her critics have argued that Cody would be unable to understand why he had to say "please" and "thank you" since he wouldn't know what they meant.

Kathie Lee: "All the more reason for him to learn to say them so that it will become second nature to him." And she added, "This is the way I was brought up."

And Kathie Lee understands the value of spending as much time as possible with her children. She believes that in doing so the children will imitate her actions and grow up to be like her, rather than like their peers, who might not have such a good role model to follow. Also, by neglecting them, she would signal that other things were more important to her than her children. And that is simply not true.

In fact, she has tried to involve her kids in her career as much as possible. For instance, she included both of them in her Christmas special in 1994 called *Kathie Lee . . . Looking for Christmas*.

The reason is obvious. She doesn't like to be away from her family. "What I do has so much exposure, people think I'm doing it constantly. The truth is, I do one album a year, which takes about three days to record. I'm no longer doing Ultra Slim-Fast. I only do Revlon a few days a year, the Home Furnishings Council three days a year, and Carnival is down to one cruise a year—and Frank and the kids come too."

And no matter what her critics say, she feels she does not talk too much about her children on TV. "I think this is a perception," she admits. "During the pregnancy, and when Cody was first born, I did—we talk about our life on our show, and that was my whole life. I was a brand-new, first-time mother. Cody came with me to the studio every day. I never dreamed I'd have another baby. So, I didn't want to miss one moment with him. So, I mean, there wasn't anything to talk about, unless I talked about Cody, because I had no life outside of him."

Philbin, who happened to be present when Kathie Lee made this comment on a *Dateline* segment, quipped, "What a long year it was, too."

"Yeah," retorted Kathie Lee. "It was a long year for everybody, apparently. But you know what? I'm paid to talk about my life. And Frank and the kids are my life pretty much."

On account of her family she would like to spend more time as a human being and less time as a professional celebrity.

"I am less busy as a professional, but more busy as a human being because there's no down time anymore. I get in from an Atlantic City concert at 2 A.M. and I'm up at six when Cassidy goes, 'Mommy, Mommy.' I may collapse in another year or two, but . . ."

Frank agrees that Kathie Lee should stay home more often. She once told this anecdote about him:

"When I get an offer, Frank will say, 'Whatever they're paying you, I'll pay you more to stay home.' The only time he doesn't resent it is when it's something that's going to change the world."

Kathie Lee realizes she has a competitive overdrive mechanism somewhere inside her that pushes her to her limits, even though she really would like to spend more time with her family.

"I wish I were a little less ambitious, frankly. My problem is that now I don't have the time to pursue things the way I did when I didn't have someone at home whom I adore. My challenge is to balance it all in a healthy way. And I'm not always successful at that."

She can't help it if she loves to work and loves its monetary compensations. And she resents the critics who claim she spends too much time dwelling on her family and not enough time on her television career.

"I'd like to see those television critics run a corporation like I do *and* be a performer, mommy, wife, friend, and contributor to society *and* go in front of the cameras live, juggling Carl Sagan one minute and Carrot Head the next."

With her material success in her career and her emphasis on the importance of a tightly knit family group, Kathie Lee knows exactly what she is and where she fits into the firmament of show business and the public mind.

"I've done a pretty good job at building an image I'm proud of. I don't need anyone baby-sitting me in my career choices. It was all about power. [Through the years] I've gotten tougher."

She feels it is essential for her to contribute something to the world as well as for her to bring up her kids as best she can. She wants to make the world a better place, not only for her own kids but for everyone.

With the kind of celebrity she has, and the job she does, she is able to harness a great deal of power for good in the world. She has discovered that she is very adept at raising money for good causes as well as raising people's awareness of evils that should be taken care of. Even so, she draws the line at taking care of the children of others.

Her job, she realizes, is to take care of her *own* children. By being all over the place looking after the rest of the world's kids, her own might grow up to become juvenile delinquents. If that happened, she would know she had failed. And she doesn't want her own children to grow up that way.

The problem is that she hates making the decision between her career and her family. "You know, Frank is twenty-three years older than me, so it's not as if we have forever. We have five grand-children who are all older than our children. You know, nothing in life prepares you for that. You hear about it, but you never think it's going to happen to you."

Kathie Lee would much rather talk about her family than talk about one of the subjects reporters barrage her with—namely, feminism. But she always manages to come up with an answer that satisfies her interviewers and sends them away knowing that little has changed in her own ideas about what it is to be a woman.

Kathie Lee does not suffer fools gladly—it's one thing she has never learned to do. "I'm a very open person. I share the real me. I've learned to live with criticism. I'm comfortable in my own skin."

There is a dark side, however, that attends her penchant for seeking out publicity for herself and her entire family. To her grief, she learned about that dark side from one Richard Jones in 1994.

Jones allegedly stalked her before being sent to jail on an unrelated charge. Even while in jail in Gastonia, North Carolina, Jones mailed threatening letters to Kathie Lee Gifford. One letter asked the devil for guidance on how to wed her for the purpose of impregnating her.

According to *Hard Copy*, Jones is a "madman who stalked Kathie Lee and turned her life into a nightmare."

Interviewed on the show, the stalker said, "I don't wanna go out there and sacrifice her children to Satan, or her husband or take her off and ravage and rape her in a mountain-top cabin."

Kathie Lee didn't learn she was being stalked by Jones until the 1993 Miss America Pageant in Atlantic City. During their investigation of Jones for the raping of his aunt, North Carolina police were searching his house and stumbled onto a chilling scrapbook compiled by Jones. It was filled with photographs of Kathie Lee Gifford. The scrapbook convinced authorities that Kathie Lee should be warned about this certifiable nut and should indeed have reason to fear for her life.

From his prison cell, Jones continues to chill her blood with such statements as "I need to make her my wife and have her bring to this world my child."

He told reporters, "What you're sayin' is I'm paranoid, delusional, crazy, and nuts—but competent to stand trial."

Furthermore, he claimed to be stalking Kathie Lee not for herself but for the United States government. It was the feds, he said, who instigated the whole thing. He *knew* what they were doing because he *watched* them do it.

"First off, I sat there and monitored radios, listened to the frequency, listened to the guys talk. I watched the feds go in the house. I watched them walk up to the door, spray this stuff on her window, everybody goes to sleep, take her out, carry her to her van with a medical unit in it. Three doctors, four doctors, three nurses. Seen them stick a thing up her nose with a needle about that freakin' long, carry her back in the house."

It sounded more like a scene from the *X Files* than from reality, but Jones apparently believes it. He claimed Kathie Lee was abducted and impregnated by government agents.

Said Jones, "I never was a stalker. I did a job with thirteen other individuals for five years. Just because she don't remember this child. . . . That's how brain implants work. Eventually she will find out the truth. Sometimes it's only a matter of time and I have plenty of time."

Kathie Lee maintained that she couldn't help it if she was famous and therefore attracted psychotic fans.

She told *Hard Copy*: "The fact that I've become famous is something I never expected. I think it's wonderful to make your living doing what you love to do. Sometimes it's pretty rotten to be a celebrity; there is not a whole lot of love about that."

Jones believed that Kathie Lee's life was still in peril—due to the government surveillance on her.

"Like I told her," he said from his jail cell, "if she looked around a little bit and noticed some of the vans parked on the street and people following her at work and back, her million-dollar fortress only protects her while she's there and she's still being monitored, just like she was."

Kathie Lee refused to kowtow to Jones's psychotic ramblings. She vowed not to live in fear of this deranged man. "I'm not going to let any human being take away the job that I have in my life. Or the pleasure in what I have after working over thirty years now for it."

Nevertheless, she said she intended to watch Jones's case closely when he came up for trial in early 1995 to see if he was found guilty and put away in jail for the rest of his life.

She was unprepared for the surprising revelation that occurred in the courthouse in Gaston County, North Carolina. It was there that Jones's aunt rose to testify against her nephew. He was being held in jail on ten counts, including five for raping his aunt, for kidnapping her, and for committing armed robbery at her house.

But it was the *appearance* of the aunt that brought surprised comments from reporters covering the trial. She was a sixty-year-old woman, but she was spry and precise when she got up to testify to her nephew's acts.

Although the ages were years apart, most observers could see a striking resemblance between the sixty-year-old aunt and Kathie Lee Gifford.

She had the same auburn hair, a reporter noted, the same high cheekbones and dark eyes, and the same petite, neat look.

Nevertheless, Kathie Lee held steadfast to her original plan not to let this man and his antics frighten her in any way.

"I do not let people like that spoil my life," she told the *Ladies Home Journal* in 1994. "You can't talk about faith and then not live up to it. You have to leave certain things up to God and you have to trust. I don't give in to fear." She struggled. "You learn to deal with it."

What annoyed Kathie Lee was that one of the tabloid TV shows had featured the story of the trial and of Jones's subsequent conviction for kidnapping and rape of his aunt. It was the way the producers had featured her that had irritated Kathie Lee.

"I have not spent one moment of my life in fear," she was quoted by Jim Jerome in the *Journal* in 1995. "When it's my time to go, the Lord will decide it, nobody else. But tabloid TV continues to sell their stupid shows—usually in sweeps periods—to hammer home that I'm terrified, living in fear.

"It's laughable, ludicrous. Why give this lunatic one second of notoriety? I'm not going to let *anybody* destroy the happiness I have found now. These [stalkers] thrive on fear, it's what gets 'em going. The only thing I fear is when, like last weekend, my baby had a 104 degrees Fahrenheit fever for three days running. *That's* terrifying."

In the end, Kathie Lee did watch as much of the trial as she could on television. And there she learned finally that Richard Jones had been sentenced to life imprisonment by the North Carolina courts. With that, Kathie Lee could breathe a silent prayer of thanks.

But the episode with the North Carolina stalker had taught Kathie Lee a lesson. With Cody, she realized, she had made a mistake in the intensity of his exposure to the public and to the press. She vowed *not* to overexpose Cassidy Erin to the press the way she had done with her boy.

Kathie Lee believes there is such a thing as getting too much publicity—and in a way it probably inspired the stalker to zero in on her. Cassidy Erin "will not be featured in the media the way Cody was," she says. "I don't want this baby to become a target for the press. I'd like her life to be a little more private."

She would bring up Cassidy Erin in the same manner that her mother brought her up, she told *Family Circle* in 1993. "While my mother was pregnant with my sister Michie, she didn't want me to be jealous. She would always say, 'When our baby comes, we'll give our baby a bath.' I felt included. That's the key. You don't abandon one child for the next. You include children in each other's lives."

In 1993 Kathie Lee revealed her secrets of motherhood:

The year is 1982. Frank Gifford, now ABC sports commentator, poses with his fiancee, Kathie Lee Johnson, on ABC's *Good Morning America*. They talked about their wedding plans to an eager audience. (*AP/Wide World Photos*)

Regis Philbin, the helper and foil of *The Joey Bishop Show*, goes over the upcoming routines with Bishop, right, on the set of the ABC-TV studio in Hollywood, California. (*AP/Wide World Photos*)

Before the rise to fame and fortune—Kathie Lee Gifford, special correspondent for *Good Morning America* and substitute for Joan Lunden as cohost with David Hartman. (*Photofest*)

Today a superstar—but it started with TV shows such as the old favorite *Hee Haw*. Kathie (on right) as a Hee Haw Honey. (*Photofest*)

Regis playing like a quarterback on the popular morning show. (*Adam Scull, Globe Photos, Inc.*)

Regis and wife, Joy, adding smiles and glamour to the occasion. (*Bill Crespinel, Globe Photos, Inc.*)

Regis and Kathie Lee announce they will host the Seventy-first Miss America Pageant, 1991. (*AP/Wide World Photos*)

Regis celebrates thirty years on TV surrounded by Kathie Lee, wife, Joy, Mary Hart, Sarah Purcell and Ann Abernathy. (*AP/Wide World Photos*)

Regis and Kathie Lee have every right to laugh—because America laughs right along with them every television morning. (*AP/Wide World Photos*)

Kathie Lee models for charity at Sotheby's to benefit Irvington House Institute for Medical Research. (*AP/Wide World Photos*)

Kathie Lee holds Lifetime Achievement Award presented to husband, Frank Gifford, by the Secretary of Housing, Jack Kemp, also a football legend like Gifford, and former Giant star Charlie Connerly. (*AP/Wide World Photos*)

Regis in a tub full of bubbles as the TV audience bubbles over with laughter. (*Adam Scull, Globe Photos, Inc.*)

Kathie Lee enjoys watching Regis and guests work out on the show. (*Photofest*)

Kathie Lee Gifford wearing football legend Frank Gifford's jersey as Regis laughs and plays along. All part of the daily fun of the nation's number one morning show. (*Photofest*)

"I always give equal doses of love and discipline. Consistency is crucial if you don't want to lose credibility;

"I tell Cody immediately when he's done something wrong and explain my reasons for disciplining him;

"I don't sugarcoat the problem;

"Once my kids are older, they'll have chores to give them a sense of responsibility;

"I never let Cody go to sleep believing that I'm angry with him. The last thought I want him to have is that he's loved."

She feels that her husband Frank is a perfect father for her children. When they discovered that Cody would be a boy, and she had been hoping for a girl, she learned how perfect a person her husband Frank was.

"I remember Frank saying to me one night, 'Honey, maybe it's better that it's a boy, because he'll be here to take care of you when I'm gone.' And that really devastated me, because I don't like to think of my husband as ever being gone. He's unbelievably fit and robust, so I never think of him as growing older to the point that he'll someday probably pass away before I do. But that's the way he thinks. 'She'll have a son who'll take care of her.' It really represents the kind of human being I'm married to."

As for Cody, Frank believes the child looks just like him. "We have the same profile."

Kathie Lee agrees. "Except Frank's nose has been broken four times. We want Cody to play gentleman sports—no boxing, no football, no hockey. As his mother, I'd like to protect his face."

When introduced on *Live With Regis and Kathie Lee*, Cody gave the show its highest New York City share of viewers up to that time—41 percent.

The entire Gifford clan lives in a colossal farmhouse in rustic Greenwich, Connecticut. Kathie Lee frequently gushes over her home. She likes it because it is strictly "country." And it's cozy, too. Eclectic, what's more. The four-poster beds are out of another era, but the sofas are very now. But it's the pillows that are her pride and joy.

The Giff isn't fascinated by the plethora of pillows. "You can't sit down because there are so many pillows on everything. It takes you ten minutes to get the pillows off the beds."

Since they moved in, there have been a number of decorators in the place. The Giff: "We've done nothing but decorate, redecorate, tear down, and build. I've had it. If [she brings] out one more decorating plan, it's over."

The glitzy farmhouse is decorated every year for Christmas as the Giffords throw a party for seventy-five guests who gather around the grand piano and sing Christmas carols. Before that, they all feast on turkey, yams, mashed potatoes, stuffing, and *klinga*, a Swedish pastry cooked according to a recipe concocted by Frank's mother.

Kathie Lee doesn't like to gloat over her inordinate wealth and palatial house. She wants the little people to think of her as one of them.

She confessed to *McCall's* in December 1991, "That's the challenge. I always think of how I can humanize things to the average person—to do it in a way that pokes fun at itself and doesn't create envy. My mom and dad came from nothing. I am very grateful for all my blessings. I don't gloat. That would be cruel."

That may sound condescending, according to her critics, but Kathie Lee doesn't live her life to please her critics. In that respect it's like her work. "People will love it, the critics will hate it. That's the story of my life. But that's okay. I may not be everyone's cup of tea, but I might be someone's glass of champagne."

The most important thing in her life is to make certain her children experience a childhood like hers, a "warm fuzzy bubble that didn't burst for years."

Not satisfied with two children of her own, Kathie Lee has considered adopting more youngsters. "All my life I'd had this rainbow-coalition concept in my mind. Wouldn't it be wonderful to adopt a hundred kids, all from different parts of the world?"

She couldn't be happier about her family even as it is. "My life is so sweet now. I'm so embarrassed by the blessings I have. Enough is enough."

Now that she has a family she must take that into consideration every time she makes a decision about her career.

"In the past I've always done what was best for me. Now I've got to do the best thing for my family. That's not necessarily the best thing for me. I'm not looking at it as some huge sacrifice. What I get from my family will long outlast any career benefits."

9

Regis as Patient:

Reege Faces the Grim Reaper

R egis Philbin is a physical fitness fanatic. He takes a daily workout at Radu, a New York gym that caters to hard-bodied çelebrities like Cindy Crawford. Candice Bergen has also been known to grace the gym from time to time and share Hollywood gossip with Radu, the Romanian owner and muscle maven.

Frequently Philbin likes to brag about his tight abs to Kathie Lee during the morning's host chat. His fantastic sixty-year-old physique is his favorite hobbyhorse, which he rides almost as frequently as he does his second: Notre Dame football.

On one memorable *Live With Regis and Kathie Lee* he stripped down to a tank top and track trunks and did pushups with Nitro and Zap of the *American Gladiators* TV series. This led one not particularly ardent admirer of Philbin to write in his newspaper column: "Regis Philbin in a tank top! The mind boggles!"

To harden his muscles, Regis was in the habit of taking pointers from his weight-lifting coach Boris Dyskin. With Dyskin, Regis worked out every day on a set schedule. He was doing "sets of

150-pound bench presses"—that is, lying on his back and lifting the weights up and away from his chest. Meanwhile, he had been experiencing a chronic annoyance—a kind of bothersome tightness in his chest. Regis hoped that his chest problem was simply a side effect of his bench presses.

And then, quite suddenly, one day something went horribly wrong. The chest pains settled into his upper body and wouldn't let go.

Not that there hadn't been any warning signals. For some time before the chest pains came on him, he had been feeling twinges, pressure, a tightening of the muscles here and there, and a definite heaviness in his chest. Philbin had always prided himself on being a realist, but in this situation he was exactly the opposite.

He *says* he just thought the pains would go away. It was more than that. He pretended to himself that they didn't exist at all. The point was, they did *not* go away. He admitted later that he could feel them at night when he was supposed to be asleep. And then, even during the daytime, he would feel them at odd moments.

Later on he did admit that at one point he thought, "Maybe it's my heart!" The thing to have done at that juncture was to go see his doctor. But instead he lapsed into pretense once again, screened off the warning that his body had given him, and ignored the pain.

Actually, Regis was faced with a rather desperate dilemma any man who believes he is healthy faces when he suddenly begins to suspect that he is not as healthy as he had always thought he was.

The pain *did* go away. But then it sneaked back. Only to disappear again! After all, something so uncertain wasn't anything *urgent*. It would work itself out, he thought.

In the back of his mind, however, a lurking shadow of doubt began to emerge. Regis was aware that our genes tie us to our forebears. His father had died of a heart attack. Regis himself had a high cholesterol count. He knew that heart attacks are hereditary, and high cholesterol counts are hereditary. All of these were defi-

nite warning signs that Philbin was too stubborn to heed. And the
lurked in the background as the pains continued to come and go

In January 1993 he was shooting a Carnival Cruise Lines com
mercial with Kathie Lee on a ship off Miami when suddenly the
pain in his chest became so intolerable that he checked himsel
into the ship's infirmary. The ship's doctor advised him to go t
the hospital onshore for more tests right away.

"You must not fly back to New York. You've got to go t
Mount Sinai Hospital down there in Miami Beach when we doc
tomorrow."

Regis called his wife, Joy. "Don't be alarmed," he told he
"I've had some chest pains for quite a while now, and it reache
an intense stage on the ship."

Joy was beside herself. She said, "Why didn't you tell me this?"

Regis hemmed and hawed. "Well, I thought I mentioned it—
in passing."

Even though he had been doing his exercises regularly, he
hadn't been doing them correctly. One of the many mistakes he
made was in not doing aerobic exercises, even though his train
ers had strongly urged him to do so.

It took a white-knuckle ride on a gurney to the cardiac treat
ment room in Miami Beach's Mount Sinai Medical Center for hin
to realize that he was seriously ill.

"They rolled me into the emergency room. They put the
camera up my groin muscle right inside my heart, showed me
where the blockage was. I *saw* it."

The sight that further convinced Regis that he might be or
the verge of death was the ghastly sight of a catheter stuck into
the artery in his groin. As he could only look on in horror, he
watched a monitor that recorded the catheter burrowing its way
into the center of his heart and a balloon (used in angioplasty
clearing away the dark spot of a clogged artery.

The doctor said, "Do you want to do it now? Or do you want
to wait?"

Philbin later confessed to Larry King, "I didn't realize the gravity of the whole thing, because on my way in, they had me on this gurney and I'm fooling around and being a wise guy, and I guess I should have realized it was a lot more serious.

"However, I *did* sober up when I saw that blockage in my artery. . . . But I realized that there was a possibility of a small percentage of these things ending up in a stroke situation, and of course they told me that in between thirty and forty percent of these angioplasties the fibers just close up again in the artery, and there's very little you can do about it. Sometimes it takes a second and a third angioplasty."

The term "angioplasty," he learned later, refers to plastic surgery on the blood vessels, usually on the inside surfaces. They were going to clean out the inside surface of his main artery.

There was only one answer to the doctor's question, "Do the angioplasty now? Or wait?"

Regis squirmed. "Do it now!"

He later recalled his thoughts at the time of the operation; they were not at all lofty ones. They were low-grade, fearful, sweat-it-out thoughts. As he lay there helpless, plugged into all that high-tech medical equipment, he knew that the odds were against him. He definitely might not make it this time.

Like anyone else in the same position, he found himself plunged into a kind of murky sadness. He might never see his family again. Then he would never know how his kids turned out. And he would miss everybody that he worked with on *Live*—Kathie Lee, Gelman, and all the rest of them. They were part of his family, too.

He was scared to death, but it could have been worse. Philbin's religious faith came to his rescue at that point. He believes in God. He believes in a heaven and a hell. His belief bolstered his faith and helped him to be less frightened than he would have been if he had had nothing to grab onto.

The doctors had carted him away to the hospital so fast that

Joy had no opportunity to be with him during this fateful operation. She was still in New York trying to get a flight to Florida when he was wheeled into the operating room at the Miami hospital.

Nevertheless, the operation went well, and he was given a clean bill of health, with the usual recommendations and warnings. Under the current rules of hospital stays, he was out in less than forty-eight hours.

And so, on January 26, two days after his angioplasty, Philbin flew back to New York to convalesce. He felt so good on the following Monday that he returned to do his show as ten million viewers, some two million more than usual, watched—apparently fascinated by Philbin's narrow escape from death. Get-well cards, flowers, and phone calls deluged the studio.

Regis was bowled over. "Don Rickles called. He was raving, 'Come on. Sweeps are here. That's what you're doing this for—publicity!' Jerry Lewis called. The apartment was full of lilies. I thought, 'This is probably the way it would have looked if I didn't make it.'"

After his operation and all the scares that went with it, Philbin slowed down—a little. Kathie Lee said of him, "Reege used to be a lovable maniac. Now he's just lovable."

Philbin responded, "Maybe I'll be my old lovable maniac self again. But right now I'm just thrilled to be around."

True to his word, Philbin soon returned to being Reege the Wildman, *out of control*! His halcyon days after the operation were short-lived. Within weeks he was catching a pass from Dallas Cowboys quarterback Troy Aikman on the stage. Guesting on the Letterman show, Philbin ran up and down the stairs, giving Letterman pause. "Should Regis really be doing this?" wondered the somewhat consternated Letterman.

In no time at all he was back to ranting as much as he had been in his preoperation days. "And what are you going to do on *your wedding night?*" he roared at a sixtyish lady who got married on his stage.

"I feel terrific," he acknowledged. "What concerns me now is that 30 to 40 percent of people who go through this go through it again, because the scarring tissue adheres to itself and plaque grows back." "Plaque" is medicalese for a deposit on the inside surface of the blood vessel. "I'm hoping I don't have to do it again, but at least I know what the procedure is."

Philbin admitted he was embarrassed by the whole episode. "I've always held myself up as a guy who exercised. Sure, I was going to work out on my abs, but I wasn't exercising right. The most important muscle of all—my heart—left me with a little egg on my face."

He went on. "This was a warning, and a close call."

To heed the warning, Philbin made plans to watch his diet very closely. "I'm taking my anticholesterol drug every day. I'm taking half an aspirin a day, and my vitamins, which I always took. Fatty dairy products are out; skim milk is in. Lots of vegetables. I can have lean red meat occasionally. Every two weeks I can have a steak."

Perhaps most important of all, he altered his gym habits. From intense, hard workouts, he switched to a more simple routine. He was much more into aerobics now than he had ever been before. He was scheduled to do from twenty to twenty-five minutes of aerobics on the bicycle and treadmill. For the other twenty to twenty-five minutes he would do what he had usually been doing before the operation.

And certain foods had to go. No hamburger. No bacon. No eggs. That was a bad loss. Philbin loved to munch bacon, especially on weekends. And he would certainly miss dipping that lobster into butter!

The week Philbin returned to the show, fit as a fiddle, he began to air public service messages about heart problems. During the entire week he kept yelling, "Regis Lives!" to punctuate his dialogue with Kathie Lee. His proclamation may have sounded like boasting, but Philbin felt he should do something to wake up other people to the dangers of heart trouble. In truth, Philbin was shy about such matters. He did not really like to shout "Regis

Lives!" It was tantamount to bragging to people how great he was. Besides, it looked much worse in print when it came out in the supermarket tabloids—and they were full of the story of his operation and its consequences.

While Philbin was in the hospital, Frank Gifford substituted for him on the show. Frank told his wife Kathie Lee that New England Patriots coach Bill Parcells had undergone an operation just like Philbin's. Kathie Lee responded by admonishing the audience to "listen to your body."

"I think this has been frightening to [Regis]," the Giff added. He "likes the extra pat of butter on his bread" and "eats a hamburger every day" for lunch. Or used to.

As it turned out, Philbin's medical problems were far from over. In May 1993, four months after the angioplasty operation, he checked into the hospital, complaining of a "heaviness" in his heart. Before he left for the hospital he videotaped a message to be broadcast on *Regis and Kathie Lee*:

"It's just a little heaviness, not anything like last time, but enough to make me call my doctor. He urged me to come in so we can take a little picture to check it out.

"I hate going through this. But I'm fine, really. I mean, who's in better shape than me? What Frank Gifford would give to look like this! So, please, no calls, no flowers, no cards. I'm fine. I'll be back on the show Monday."

According to Gelman, Philbin felt the heaviness as he walked to his treadmill to work out. "He was mad at himself because he thinks he made too much of the heaviness."

Nevertheless, Philbin was right to check into the hospital. This time he needed an atherectomy, a follow-up procedure to his angioplasty operation. "Atherectomy" refers to a surgical cleaning out of a fatty accumulation inside an artery.

After the atherectomy, Regis boasted, "I'm pain-free. [Before] I'd have this [recurring] pain . . . I was hoping it would be a muscle pull. I was hoping it was any number of things. I frankly denied it to myself and everybody around me."

His current regimen substitutes walking for aerobics and makes other adjustments to his old routine.

"The aerobics didn't mean anything," he has said. "So I started walking, and came to find out that I really enjoy it. I walk for the first twenty or thirty minutes. This is what I do now every other day. Then I do my weights. In the past, all I did was my weights, but now, I think I'm on track with the right workout for me."

Philbin could even wax sentimental about the weights.

"There's such a terrific feeling when you get through with a weight workout. I don't know, psychologically you feel terrific. It's a great high. All the endorphins kicking in. I've always felt that way about it, and I really do love it. Sometimes it's tough to get down there because it really *is* work."

To celebrate his recovery he decided to make an exercise video as a message about heart awareness and the importance of exercise for good health. "In a couple of weeks I will make my exercise video. The 100,000th video of its kind."

He now realized that simply lifting weights was not enough. You needed aerobic exercise to boot. "Finally, I've seen the light. Now that I am more or less forced to do it, I'm enjoying it a lot."

His original problem was a simple one. "I was not exercising my heart. I never jogged, walked, or used a Stairmaster." After his doctor told him what was wrong, Philbin said, "I found out how much I'd been missing. I wish I could jump-start everybody."

Which is the reason he planned his video: *Regis Philbin: My Personal Workout.*

Even so, it takes a bit of doing for anyone to get ready to perform a proper exercise.

"You've got to get yourself psyched up to get into that gym and do it, but I do enjoy it, and what we did on the video was, we reduced everything to just plain old simple dumbbells. Hey, you can do it without any weights at all, or you can do it with very light dumbbells, or if you're really into it, you can use your own dumbbells and take a good workout."

As for the workout video, Regis explains: "People [had been] asking me about doing a video like that, but I had always declined, because there were so many exercise videos out there. It was the blockage that changed my mind. [Afterward] I went on the show and talked about my situation and I'd get calls and letters from people that said, 'Hey, you saved my life.' They had changed their lifestyles, too. So I decided to do it."

Drawing on some eight million viewers a day, *Live* helped boost the sales of the video he made. At least, Regis felt, the video itself helped hundreds of thousands of people begin to pay attention to their bodies and exercise their hearts as well as all their other muscles.

In a way, it was a kind of public service message in color. At least that was the way he began to feel about it.

10

Regis and Kathie Lee as Body-Builders:

The Workout Videos

Regis Philbin's exercise video is unlike most other workout videos in that his does not feature a score of people jumping up and down in a gym as music is piped in to accompany them.

In fact, Philbin makes the theme of his video clear at its outset: He is doing nothing more than showing you how he exercises to keep his heart in healthy condition. He is not *ordering* you to do this exercise or you'll die; he is merely telling you how he keeps his own heart in good shape.

The video also stresses that you should not do any of the exercises until you consult your doctor. Otherwise, the video has a very relaxed feel to it—exactly like *Live With Regis and Kathie Lee.*

Throughout the tape Regis keeps passing on good advice from his doctor. "I was a big red meat man. My doctors told me I was going to have to watch my diet and get into aerobics."

He exhorts the viewer in his video: "You're going to be up! You're going to be strong! You're going to be ready for anything!"

Making no false promises, he says: "I can't guarantee you're going to get your own morning show. But if you ever meet Kathie Lee you'll be strong enough to handle her."

Regis: My Personal Workout is in almost every way a kind of public service message, as Philbin devotes the first fifteen minutes to proselytizing about the need for a shipshape heart. To accomplish that goal, he says, you would be well advised to practice aerobics.

As Regis has said elsewhere: "I regret that I didn't get started on aerobics earlier."

For an excellent aerobic exercise, Philbin suggests walking. "I was told that, really, I needed to do this. So I started walking, and I love it. I think I have more stamina, more endurance, even enough to handle Kathie Lee in the morning."

Most of the videotape concerns Philbin's weight-lifting routine, but there are also segments that star Kathie Lee, Regis's wife, Joy, and Gelman, who demonstrate the proper use of the Stairmaster, the treadmill, walking, and the stationary bicycle.

There isn't much in the way of entertainment until toward the end of the tape. Then weight workouts for beginners are trotted out, interspersed with comic bits. In one of them, Regis lifts weights in front of David Letterman's studio and says, "I bet David Letterman can't do this."

The exercise section of the tape is divided into two parts, aerobic and muscle building. For part one, Philbin learns aerobics from Kathie Lee and Joy as he watches them exercise. Part two has Philbin doing his own exercising, lifting weights in his home gym, demonstrating exercises for all the muscles of the body.

A message near the beginning of the video says you need to exercise your heart to stay healthy. After the message leaves the screen, we see Philbin standing in a black sweatshirt in front of a brown lake in Central Park.

He launches into a story about what a skinny youth he was

as he grew up in New York, showing the viewer black-and-white photographs of himself as a teenager. To build himself up he worked out with weights. He continued weight lifting when he attended Notre Dame. He worked out under the guidance of Father Lang, the fourth strongest man in the world.

Philbin then informs the viewer that he took up aerobics after he suffered a blocked artery. Another man in sweats walks on the scene and Regis greets him. It turns out he's Philbin's walking trainer. The trainer explains to Philbin how he should walk and the two of them set out on a hike, their pace slow at first.

The trainer tells Philbin he should walk for about twenty to thirty minutes at a healthy clip to get his heart pumping. Walking three times a week is good for your circulation. The key points to learn are that when you start your walk, maintain a slow pace, then gradually increase it.

Next, Regis leaves the trainer and walks into a building, where he finds Kathie Lee walking on a treadmill. She is wearing dark baggy shorts and dark tights. Philbin asks her how to use the treadmill. She explains as she exercises on it. Then, as Regis leaves, Kathie Lee yells after him: "He's the greatest! He's the king!"

Regis walks down the steps into the basement and meets his wife, Joy, who is working out on a Stairmaster. He asks her how to exercise on it. She answers and tells him she usually works out for fifteen minutes at a time. She is dressed in black too, and we see the weights lying behind her in the background of the Philbins' home gym. The Philbins kiss.

The next person he meets is Gelman, who is riding a stationary bicycle. Regis asks him how to use it. Gelman fills him in and Philbin departs.

That is the end of the aerobics segment. As yet, other than walking, we haven't seen the health fiend starred in the video do a single exercise.

That all changes in the second half of the tape. It's Philbin's turn to work out. Alone in his home gym, wearing a blue tank top with his sweat pants, he gives a lecture on the use of weights.

He then presents his list of "Startup Strength Programs," which he demonstrates by doing warm-up exercises on the dark hardwood floor, a brick wall behind him. He performs different types of warm-ups with Muzak playing softly in the background.

The music is relaxing and low-key as is Philbin when he speaks. However, his huffing and puffing during each exercise makes him sound like a very old man with asthma and his heavy breathing commences to grate on one's nerves. Too, he appears to be molting before our very eyes, his skin splotchy and chapped.

After he finishes his warm-up, he exercises different parts of his body, starting with his torso. He executes a dozen-odd push-ups and then is joined by his weight-lifting trainer, Debbie White. Before she leaves, she hands him some dumbbells as he lies on his back on a long bench-pressing table.

Then his back gets a workout. He performs "Standing Reverse Flies." Then he exercises his shoulders and drinks a little mineral water from a plastic bottle. It's good to drink water between exercises, he says. Then he exercises his arms, legs, and buttocks. The exercising of his abs (abdominal muscles, for the uninitiated) is next. You can't have tight abs unless you exercise them.

And that's the end of the forty-seven minute tape, save for the irritating commercial for Harvest Crisps crackers tacked onto it at the end.

One newspaper video critic, Michelle Nicolosi, panned the tape mostly on account of Regis Philbin's looks. She found him "funny looking." Also he "seems to have shaved his underarms." She was annoyed—or perplexed that his head and chest hair were not the same color. And, to top it off, she said, he looked lousy in a "U-shirt."

If that wasn't enough, she found his "pasty flesh" hard to take. Practically the only good thing about the tape, as far as she was concerned, was that Philbin was such a mess to look at that he "must make exercisers feel better about themselves than staring at hard bodies does."

The *Kansas City Star* critic also gave it a thumbs-down, entertainment-wise: "Anyone who buys this video for entertainment purposes probably will be disappointed." The critic failed to find the humor in Regis's "expounding on the use of dumbbells: 'Switch to the other arm! You can't have one arm bigger than the other! Come on!'"

Another critic felt ripped off after he purchased the video because it was filled with static and had blurry resolution. He got a better picture with the rabbit ears on his TV set. Nor did he appreciate plunking down twenty dollars for a tape that forced him to sit through a commercial for Harvest Crisps crackers presented by Philbin and his wife. Wasn't the whole point of buying a video the fact that you didn't have to watch commercials?

Funny? No. Easy to take? Yes. At least you don't get yelled and screamed at by a gym teacher doing his impersonation of Genghis Khan, as you do on some of the exercise videos.

Once the Regis Philbin *Workout* video appeared, it was almost inevitable that there might be a repeat by Regis's close associate on the *Live* show. And, sure enough, in the summer of 1994 who should have an exercise video but Kathie Lee?

It was called the *Feel Fit and Fabulous Workout* video.

A warning: If you want comedy, don't bother to view Kathie Lee's *Fit and Fabulous Workout* video. This is a tape for those who like to watch a bunch of women jumping up and down to monotonous Muzak for almost an hour that never seems to end.

At the beginning of the tape the viewer is warned that the following exercises are not for everyone. The idea is to check with your doctor if you have any misgivings about them. After this introduction, Kathie Lee is on the screen in her silk-stocking living room where she proceeds to launch into a lecture on a "full body workout."

She maintains that she has always detested exercising. "In the past, I hated even the thought of exercising, much less actually getting out there and doing it. But now, after two babies and hitting forty, I realize it's not only the best thing I can do for

119

me, but also for my family. I'm happier, more confident and I have more stamina to face the challenge of the workplace and motherhood."

Sounds similar to Regis Philbin's exercise video in which he claims that the viewer will have enough energy to face Kathie Lee in the morning if the exercises in his tape are performed. The difference is that Regis makes a stab at humor, whereas Kathie Lee does not.

As already mentioned, there's little comedy in Kathie Lee's tape (which in the long run is much like her cohost Philbin's). Most of the dialogue is spoken by a physical fitness expert who, like a female drill sergeant, barks orders at Kathie Lee and her friends to exercise.

In her introduction, Kathie Lee goes on to say, "In this exercise video, I think we have succeeded in making fitness fun. So join me, my sister Michie and good friends Denise and Laurie as fitness expert C. B. Yelverton, M.S., shows us how to feel fit and fabulous." (It is not quite clear *what* "M.S." stands for.)

The production values of Kathie Lee's tape are much better than Regis's. The resolution is good and there is no annoying static throughout the tape. Alas, the same cannot be said of Philbin's. The music is as redundant and boring to listen to as the exercises are to watch.

In the next scene Kathie Lee has changed into green leotards to prepare for exercising. She is now in a home gym. In the background, tall windows almost reach to the ceiling and philodendrons are spaced about in planters. The off-white colored floor is so smooth you can see the reflections of the exercisers as they jump about on it.

Kathie Lee introduces physical fitness expert C. B. Yelverton, who wears purple leotards. Yelverton promptly tells the viewer how to determine your heart rate.

Kathie Lee explains, "We don't want anybody to get hurt."

She proceeds to introduce the two friends and her sister

Michie. They all start performing aerobics as Yelverton snaps out commands.

"Like my old cheerleading days!" cries Kathie Lee at one point.

She is quickly cut off by Yelverton who asserts that no talking is allowed during exercises. Kathie Lee pipes down after being chewed out.

For the program, the five women alternately lift weights and cool down with aerobics. The women are constantly moving, constantly bouncing up and down for some forty minutes. It's exhausting just to watch them.

Finally it's over. Yelverton commands the four women to drink water. Kathie Lee tells Yelverton she's going to the ladies room. In your face, Sarge.

For the next scene the five women each have a purple mat under them as they lie on their backs. Yelverton tells them how to exercise their abs as they lie on their backs.

Time to cool down and stretch.

They all cheer when they have finished their ordeal. The viewer wants to cheer too: the ordeal of watching them is over.

In the next scene, Kathie Lee is alone with a towel draped over her shoulders. She takes the viewer on a tour of her luxurious home. In one somewhat saccharine moment, she exercises her abs while playing with her little daughter Cassidy.

On to the kitchen. Kathie Lee uses the sink to exercise her hamstrings as she skins a carrot, a culinary process that seems foreign to her. Disgusted with the carrot, she tosses it away and admits she rarely visits the kitchen.

Cut to Cody's bedroom. Kathie Lee puts Cody to bed and lies down on a love seat. She explains how to exercise her legs and relax stress in this position.

Cut to her spacious bathroom. She is brushing her teeth. She points out that this is a good time to exercise your buttocks. As you brush, bend your legs and, on rising, squeeze your butt.

Her husband Frank, clad in a plush bathrobe fit for the sports figure that he was and still is, enters the bathroom and says suavely, "Her keeping me young is killing me."

She bats her eyelashes at him and falls into his arms, squeezing her butt.

The *New York Times* in a rundown of various exercise videos—there are scores of them—included the following on the Kathie Lee *Workout* tape.

"Ms. Gifford says she once hated the thought of exercise, but hitting forty and having two children changed her mind. This is her program for working mothers. The most inspiring part of it is her trainer, C. B. Yelverton—forty-six and a grandmother-to-be in spectacular condition.

"The class alternates weight training with basic aerobics. The postscript is a private tour of Ms. Gifford's home, including tips on how to firm up your gluteus maximus while brushing your teeth."

11

Kathie Lee as Businesswoman:
The Bottom Line

It was 1984. Kathie Lee had been doing her stint on *Good Morning America*, substituting for Joan Lunden and working on special assignments for the show since 1982. It was a good job. The people were nice to her. And yet she had a strange sense of déjà vu.

Was she repeating herself in her charade with Anita Bryant? She had to ask herself, straight on, what was she except a stand-in for Joan Lunden? What had happened to the real Kathie Lee?

In her heart she may have known it was time to leave. But by now Kathie Lee was well aware of all the pitfalls of show business; even as a newscaster and interviewer, she was touched by disappointment. She had carved a comfortable little niche for herself—but the niche was compromising and constricting, preventing her growth. Certainly it was safer to stay where she was. But was that what she really wanted?

Kathie Lee was beginning to get that old itch again to move on to better things. And yet, what was better? No matter; she began making her old familiar rounds as she had always done when she wanted to make a change of some kind. And, oddly enough, in July 1984 she found a chance that might pay off for her.

She met a man named Bob Dickinson, the president of Carnival Cruise Line. The company, a part of Norwegian Cruise Lines, had been in existence since 1972. Founded by Ted Arison, a former Norwegian Cruise Lines executive, the line was beginning as a one-ship fleet called "the flagship of the golden fleet." In fact there was no fleet.

Fate did not treat the fledgling line at all well. On its maiden cruise, the *Mardi Gras* (number one of one) carried three hundred influential travel agents on a complimentary cruise straight onto a hidden sandbar off the Florida coast where it ran aground in a most ignominious fashion. Somehow, after many hours of travail, the ship got pulled off the sand bar, was refloated successfully, and the cruise continued to its rather anticlimactic end.

Bob Dickinson, a trouble shooter for American International Travel Service of Boston, one of the investors in the Carnival Cruise Line, was called in to investigate. Dickinson flew to Florida and stayed on to become marketing vice president, working for the Arisons.

Dickinson reestablished the entire line, throwing out the high-blown concept of "flagship of the fleet" and concentrated everything on the idea of the "fun that travelers could have on board a cruise ship." It worked. By 1983, Carnival was carrying 260,000 passengers a year out of an industry total of 1.5 million—one passenger out of every six who sailed the Caribbean that year!

Dickinson began looking for someone to act as a spokesperson for the line. The list of potentials was finally boiled down to Cathy Lee Crosby, the host of *That's Incredible*, Joyce De Witt, the spunky roommate in *Three's Company*, and Kathie Lee herself.

Kathie Lee was easily the first choice, according to Dickinson. "She can sing, she can dance, she is attractive, she is perky, she is a girl-next-door type in that she is not threatening," Dickinson said, as he rattled off her obvious attributes.

He did not mention one of the most appealing of her sub-liminal strengths. She was, of course, the paradigmatic Middle American—even after all those years in show business. It came over in her appearance, and in the way she sang.

There was a straightforward quality about her, an honest, open look that brooked no nonsense. She had lots of appeal—not only to men, who found her sexy, but also to women, who reacted positively to her because she was pretty but nonthreatening.

Working with Bob Dickinson and McFarland and Drier, the ad agency in charge of the Carnival commercials, Kathie Lee immediately began searching her repertoire for a song to sing as she enjoyed herself on the cruise ship. The song they eventually decided on was "If They Could See Me Now," which was the kind of number you could belt out without being criticized as being off-key or low-brow, since the song was written to be that way anyhow.

When Carnival had started its maiden cruise, it was losing money. But by 1992, twenty years later, it was earning a net income of $276 million, on gross revenues of $1.47 billion. A great deal of the line's growth in the past decade has been due to Kathie Lee's energetic TV commercials.

Today, Carnival is the most popular cruise line in the world—true to what the company slogan claims—and it is immensely profitable. It also owns and operates a tonier version of the cruise ship in the Holland America Line. And it owns and operates the so-called yacht-concept Windstar Line.

Dickinson's view on a cruise is still the main operating concept behind the Carnival Cruise Line. "I knew nothing about the cruise business, so I reasoned we were in the vacation business," he says. "What do people want on a vacation? The most common adjective is *fun*."

It was Dickinson and Carnival who pioneered the contemporary cruise segment that boasts of such "plain folks" entertainment as singles cocktail parties, Las Vegas-style shows, poolside pillow-fight tournaments, and updated vaudevillian acts—magicians, singers, and stand-up comics—for the late hours of evening.

From the beginning of his association with Kathie Lee, Dickinson broadened the appeal of his spokesperson by adding members of her own "family"—husband Frank Gifford and talk-show cohost Regis Philbin, for example. And later on, there were Kathie Lee's two children as possible candidates.

In 1991, Carnival's campaign shifted gears slightly, featuring Kathie Lee Gifford as usual, but not in a singing and hard-pitch role. Instead, the key feature of the new campaign was a "Fun Ship" concept of a cruise vacation—dining, entertainment, health-and-fitness activities, and family togetherness.

For background this time, the McFarland and Drier commercials used the *Fantasy*, the line's biggest and newest ship, introduced in March. The commercials featured the ship's spectacular neon-lit atrium, called the Centrum, as a dramatic visual background for Kathie Lee's pitch. The set was reminiscent more of a seagoing hotel than of a cruise liner—an impression underlined by the commercial's dialogue.

Kathie Lee's success as a commercial spokesperson for Carnival Cruise Line was by no means unexpected, but it did teach her that she perhaps had a lot more potential than she thought she had. After winning the plum Carnival campaign, she tried out for others and was almost equally successful—although the campaigns were not quite so focused and intense as those Carnival produced. But she was maintaining an excellent track record; her successes added mightily to her worth as a performer and celebrity.

And, of course, she had joined Regis Philbin by this time and was helping take that show up to the top. In 1990, five years later, she signed on with the Home Furnishings Council. Actually, Home Furnishings Council was a simple promotional unit, dedicated to helping people enjoy their own homes. For example, in the first year Kathie Lee became their spokesperson the campaign theme was "It all begins at home."

Anyone interested could receive a free forty-two-page home-decorating guide called *Haven*. And there was a toll-free number to call to find retailers in the area participating in the Council's campaign.

The Home Furnishings Council was started in order to spur sales in the home-furnishings industry. In the mid-1980s, retirees and baby boomers were supposed to be spending more time at home, and more money in the stores, buying things to make them comfortable.

However, consumers were spending only as much in 1990 as they had spent in 1970. The money wasn't going to home furnishings at all, the marketing experts discovered in a series of studies. It was going to eating out, to electronics gadgets, and to new cars.

The tone of Kathie Lee's pitch in those commercials was to make the purchase of home furnishings seem to be a friendly, affable event, rather than a daunting one to those who were out shopping.

In 1991 Kathie Lee found herself some more business. That was the year after which Cody was born. It was somebody's bright idea at Ultra Slim Fast, the weight-reducing company, to amalgamate the birth of Cody with a get-thin-fast diet through Ultra Slim Fast for Kathie Lee and Frank Gifford—focusing on how fast Kathie Lee could get back into shape after the birth of her firstborn.

Kathie loved the idea. She told her audience on *Live* in great detail exactly how hard the Ultra Slim Fast people had worked—supervising Cody's nap time with a staff of at least fourteen people. The background of the commercial was fascinating.

In *Adweek*, Barbara Lippert wrote: "Unfortunately, the tantalizing story she told on the show about the making of the commercial . . . was far more interesting than the spot itself."

Several unexpected things happened during the making of the commercial. One of them was a rather mysterious weight gain in Frank Gifford—called a "sympathy weight gain" in psychological terms. And in the end it was *he* who had to take off more poundage after the birth of Cody than Kathie Lee did!

In the commercial itself, Kathie Lee was shown slipping Cody into his crib, delivering the pitch that had been written for her. Frank was waiting in the hallway. "Thanks to Ultra Slim Fast, the weight is just where it should be!" she intoned. Frank appeared, grabbing her around the waist. "Off!" concluded Kathie Lee.

In the race to reduce, Kathie Lee beat out her husband—but eventually even he got back into his usual wardrobe.

The Ultra Slim Fast commercial was shown all over the place, on every TV station in almost every market.

It was the success of Jaclyn Smith's line of women's clothes for Kmart that got Kathie Lee to thinking: "For the last seven years people have asked me about my clothes. Anybody on television gets that. It's not that I'm special. People call in and say, 'Where can I get it? How much is it?' But when they find out how expensive the clothes are, it is really prohibitive for so many people."

The point was, why not make use of the audience interest in Kathie Lee's clothes? Of course the high-end designer pieces she usually wore on the show were costly items at best. How to get them scaled down to a price that the average viewer could afford was a major sticking point for Kathie Lee.

But it was no sticking point for Bob Adler, of Halmode, a clothing manufacturer in New York City. He knew what to do immediately. One of Halmode's lines was called Plaza South, which made nurses' uniforms, maternity wear, and budget-priced sportswear.

It was the bottom-line price of the item that was most important to Kathie Lee—and to Bob Adler. Adler said he could meet the price. He would have the clothes brought in to sell at under a hundred dollars apiece.

"A six-hundred dollar suit I might wear on the show is totally prohibitive to the average person," Kathie Lee explains. "So we took the outfits I've worn that have gotten the most response from our viewers and reinterpreted them."

Kathie Lee did have certain specifications for the job she would be doing. "I wanted to have input and be involved in putting together the collection. I had been approached to be a spokes-woman of other clothing lines, but I turned down the offers. I was already a spokeswoman for Carnival Cruise Line and Ultra Slim Fast." This time, she wanted more.

"I wanted to *do* a line that reflects what we do on our show, and wanted the clothes to be affordable to the women that watch the show." She then investigated Bob Adler and Halmode and found a company that had at least twenty-eight years of integrity behind it. And so the contracts were signed and Kathie Lee joined Plaza South for a new line of clothes titled "Kathie Lee for Plaza South."

The idea was to move her into an already existent line rather than start up a brand new one—which would cost a lot of money—and see if the idea had any worth to it.

And so thirty-six new outfits in both "romance" and "career" categories were designed—using the styles of more expensive clothes as a basis for the look itself. Summer items were made of cotton and linen blends—suitable for outdoor parties, or for church, or for weddings. The selection included suits, pants, jacket outfits, and coatdresses.

Kathie Lee met frequently with the line's official designer, Vickie Felix. They would review the expensive TV clothes and think about making others like them.

Kathie Lee: "We literally take things from my wardrobe, things I like, or that get the most reaction on the air, and we reinter-pret them."

Vickie Felix sketched the new styles, and the two of them, working together, selected fabric, braids, and buttons.

During her foray into the clothing business, Kathie Lee picked up a number of manufacturing facts quickly. A lot of her line was manufactured overseas—simply because some of the lace work—Battenberg lace in particular—is a lost craft in America.

"It's not a matter of putting Americans out of work to put Orientals to work. I'd like to change that around."

She went on. "Our ratio is fifty-fifty. For the time being, I'm proud of that." She said that she would not be wearing any of the new line on the air—"unless I'm in dire need of a new outfit, simply because I don't want to use the show as a platform to market it. There's a classier way to do it."

In the end, a thousand stores handled the new line, including Lord & Taylor, Dillard's, Belk, Rich's, Macy's, and Burdines.

From its inception the line was a success. Within the first two months of its existence, the sales were good. In fact, Adler was predicting a ten-million dollar first-year gross revenue.

Kathie Lee was not particularly surprised. The success of the line was due "mostly to the economy. The economy is very bad at the moment [1992]. The last thing wives and mothers think about is themselves. It's always the child that gets the new outfit. The fact that you can get a nice outfit for yourself, for under a hundred dollars, is important to women."

Another point: "I think because of the economy, people are staying home more and watching television. It's the reason all the talk shows are doing so well." And, of course, her new line of clothing was mentioned on the show, as well as during her round of personal appearances.

When the line was introduced, Kathie Lee had butterflies, of course. "Every night before one of the launches, I would get these anxiety attacks, afraid that nobody would show up. But each time, I came away elated and rewarded by the turnout and response." And, incidentally, "We launched in a difficult economic climate, in the teeth of a recession."

There was another consideration. "There is a lesson to be learned for the retailers in that you've got to get people into the stores in order to sell them."

Adler was pleased with the reception Kathie Lee got from the women who came to see her when she appeared at several of the stores to introduce her new line.

"She has an immediate rapport with the people, which is so evident on the TV show. It's unusual for me as a manufacturer to be out in the stores, but I've learned what the power of a personal appearance and hands-on connection with the consumer can mean."

"About 1,500 women came to the store to meet her," said Lavelle Olexa, a Lord & Taylor senior vice president in Scarsdale. "Kathie Lee is charming and personable, but the best part is that the merchandise is selling very well. It's well made and well priced. The personal appearance showed immediate sales response, as [such appearances] normally do, but in her case she has continuous visibility because of the TV show, unlike many of the designers who make personal appearances."

The line was a success the first year. Still, Kathie Lee was thinking it could have been better. She met with Bob Adler and the two hashed over all the known variables. In the end, it was decided that the hundred-dollar cap was a bit high for the clothes in the Plaza South line. Therefore: let's go mass.

"I decided to go mass-market," she said, "because I wanted to be where America lives and shops."

Halmode would still be doing her line, but it would not be part of the Plaza South line, but a brand-new line: the Kathie Lee Collection.

Designing for a mass market was something Kathie Lee had to learn about before she could begin giving orders to her staff. "I have to check my taste at the door," she confessed, "and realize there's a huge market that likes different things. I like bare arms and short skirts, which make most women uncomfortable."

Even though Kathie Lee was able to squeeze back into her size 4 clothes only weeks after the birth of her second child, she insisted on including in the line maternity and large-sized dresses. There was a well-known designer who refused to design large-sized clothes; he loudly declaimed that he was a *designer*, and not an *upholsterer*.

Not so Kathie Lee: "Half the world battles the bulge. My mother, who would love to be a size twelve, is sometimes size sixteen, but she's still attractive and cares about clothes. So we make all sizes."

The Kathie Lee Collection focused initially on career sportswear and dresses in a wide range of sizes, with most outfits retailing for less than fifty dollars. Included in the line were accessories like purses. Plans for the future included outerwear, sleepwear, underwear, shoes, and children's wear.

Everything was ready for the launching of the Kathie Lee Collection in February 1995. But a preview, set up at a Wal-Mart store in Middle Village, Long Island, was one of seventeen stores that tested the Kathie Lee line early in January.

Adler was astounded at what happened. The test results were amazing. In just the first ten days, he said, 20 to 40 percent of the Kathie Lee items were gone. "It was incredible, and this was all full-priced spring merchandise while the store was running after Christmas sales."

According to Adler, the Kathie Lee Collection has the potential to exceed the sales of Jaclyn Smith for Kmart, which reportedly is now around $300 million and one of the biggest of all the private celebrity labels. The Kathie Lee Collection was slated to be shown in 2,133 stores across the country when it debuted.

"It appears it's going to be significant," Adler says. He finds Kathie Lee a "charming, witty, charismatic, and very concerned" woman. "And what could be a better advertisement for Wal-Mart than having [Kathie Lee] on TV every single day at nine in the morning?"

Using Kathie Lee Gifford, whose personality is particularly popular and attractive to Middle America, was a canny move, according to an observer of the garment industry. Besides which, performer and singer and talk-show host though she is, she is foremost an excellent, very savvy businesswoman.

These four business enterprises are not the only ones in which Kathie Lee has become interested. She also did a number of TV commercials for Revlon at one time or another. But the ones described here are her more major business arrangements.

She's so involved in these businesses that she can't always keep track of them all. And this in turn begins to worry some of her close associates.

Including the King.

Her face is so omnipresent, her TV cohost Regis Philbin tells her, that he is afraid she might become overexposed. "I worry about the overexposure factor in our business, and I'm sure she does, too. Everywhere you look, there's Kathie Lee. But I don't see any slacking off in the demand for her. She's still a hot commodity."

In addition to her flurry of activity with Carnival Cruises, Revlon, Ultra Slim Fast, the Home Furnishings Council, and her line of clothes for Halmode, she is a partner in Giff and Golda Productions, a company named after Frank Gifford and Kathie Lee (Golda is Frank's pet name for her). Their company produced Kathie Lee's 1994 Christmas special on TV. It also intends to be involved in the production of a pilot for *Kathie Lee: The Sitcom*—a project now in the hopper for CBS-TV.

It's no surprise that Kathie Lee likes to be called ambitious. "That's a good word as long as it isn't preceded by 'ruthless.' I think the people who watch our show understand the heart behind the ambition, and I am ambitious: to raise two beautiful children with good hearts, to make a difference in this world, to make my marriage healthy and sexy and joyful and lasting."

She is well aware that much of her claim to success can be attributed to her impressively clean image. She likes to call herself the "Moral Majority's Madonna." It's good to know that former gospel singers, too, can become rich and famous in America. Not only did she once sing those gospels for Oral Roberts, but for a time also for Jim and Tammy Faye Bakker and their PTL Club.

Kathie Lee believes she owes much of her success to God. "Look what I have to show for my patience and faith: a life I share with a gorgeous partner who is also my confidant, my lover, my best friend in all the world, my shrink, and the father of our [children]; a wonderful home and . . . a career burning on all jets. It's so good it's scary. I'm too happy."

As a savvy businesswoman, she knows the importance of keeping her good image untarnished. For this reason she recently wanted to have her photograph removed from a 1995 edition of *Maternity Fashion & Beauty* magazine.

Inside the magazine was an article plugging the Kathie Lee Collection. She had no problem with the cover photo or the article. Her problem stemmed from the fact that the publisher of the magazine, Larry Flynt, was the publisher of the notorious skin magazine *Hustler Busty Beauties*.

Reasoning that any association with Flynt would damage her image, Kathie Lee tried to get her lawyers to remove her photo from the cover of *Maternity Fashion & Beauty* magazine. When she had originally agreed to do the cover photo and the article for the magazine, she was not aware that Larry Flynt was its publisher. Her lawyers went over her contract with a fine-toothed comb, but could find no loopholes. She then tried to persuade the magazine's editor to remove her picture. No way.

Nor could the magazine's editor understand what all the fuss was about. After all, it was Kathie Lee who had contacted them to put her face on the cover to plug her new line of clothes in the article inside.

Editor-in-chief Linda Arroz said she never tried to conceal from Kathie Lee the fact that the magazine was published by Flynt. It just never seemed to come up in the conversation. "We didn't hide who we were. We had an agreement and we felt very strongly we had done nothing wrong."

Arroz clinched her decision to publish the photo of Kathie Lee on the cover when she came across a recent issue of *Longevity*, a magazine about health published by Bob Guccione of *Penthouse*.

"I was just so taken aback," said Arroz, with tongue planted firmly in cheek. "Here was Kathie Lee on the cover of a respected magazine owned by a so-called porn king."

Kathie Lee's photo on the little-known magazine, *Maternity Fashion & Beauty*, boosted sales up from 300,000 copies to almost half a million.

The magazine's advertising director, Susan Milano, said, "Kathie Lee is America's sweetheart, and she's doing tremendous things for us. Celebrities definitely sell."

The incident just goes to show how far Kathie Lee will go to keep her image immaculate. As far as she was concerned, it would be an unwise career move to have her name associated with Larry Flynt's in any way.

She is proud of the fact that her South Plaza line always reflected her straight-arrow image: suits in classic fabrics with gold filigree or braided trim, and dresses trimmed in Battenberg lace. As is her wont, she donates portions of her profits to charity, in this case the Variety Club International's Children's Charity.

Kathie Lee has always believed that her good fortune came to her directly from God—that is, that it was not her doing alone, by any means. And because God was good to her, and to those she loved, she would always make a great effort to give back whatever she could to help the needy and the less fortunate.

She has always been a cheerfully generous tither. She and the Giff have always been first in line to pour money into charities created to help children—especially those born with crack-cocaine addiction, or the AIDS virus.

She and her husband carry out their charity work mainly under the auspices of the Association to Benefit Children and of the Variety Club International. The Giffords' special focus is on facilities for terminally ill children and their families.

Through the above agencies, they have developed two separate facilities in New York City, donating over two million dollars to get them established.

One of them is the Variety Cody Gifford House for Children with Special Needs. It is familiarly known as "Cody House." The other is called "Cassidy's Place." One charity for each child. These agencies provide care for children who are HIV-positive or who are born addicted to crack.

The Giffords also support the Multiple Sclerosis Association and the Special Olympics. Kathie Lee was cochair with Barbara

Bush for the First Lady's literacy program for ABC-TV. A percentage of Kathie Lee's profits from her clothing line goes to charities like Paul Newman's Hole in the Wall Gang Camp and the Children's Charity. And she also donates all her book profits to children's charities. In addition, she has given money to other charitable organizations.

To sum up her business affiliations and put them all in the proper perspective, here is a checklist as of mid-1995:

1. Television Talk-Show Cohost: *Live With Regis and Kathie Lee*—five live tapings per week.

2. Endorsements: Almay, Revlon, Carnival Cruise Line, and Home Furnishings Council.

3. Clothing Line: Kathie Lee Collection (formerly Kathie Lee for Plaza South), now available at Wal-Mart stores nationwide.

4. Live Concerts: Two dates with Regis, solo nightclub act, benefit performance.

5. Exercise Video: *Kathie Lee's Feel Fit and Fabulous Workout*, released in 1994.

6. Guest Television Spots: *Evening Shade, Seinfeld, The Late Show with David Letterman, The Tonight Show*.

7. Television Specials: *Kathie Lee . . . Looking for Christmas*, and others in the works.

8. Record Albums: *Sentimental* and *It's Christmastime*.

9. Books Authored: *The Quiet Riot*, 1976; *I Can't Believe I Said That!*, 1992; *Listen to My Heart*, 1995.

10. Books Coauthored (with Regis Philbin): *Cooking With Regis and Kathie Lee*, 1993; *Entertaining With Regis and Kathie Lee*, 1994.

11. Television Sitcom: A pilot for her own sitcom is currently in preparation, possibly to air in the fall of 1995.

12. Cohost: Miss America Pageant.

12

Kathie Lee as Wife:
The Giff on Kathie Lee

According to Frank "the Giff" Gifford, it was love at first sight.

As he tells it, "I first met Kathie Lee Johnson in 1982. I was filling in for David Hartman on *Good Morning America* and Kathie was in early that morning to do an entertainment segment."

There was the Giff at his dressing room table, struggling with his contacts, clad informally in his jeans. And it was the jeans, apparently, that caught the eye of Kathie Lee. In the future she would often say that the sight of his backside there gave new meaning to the football phrase "tight end."

"All I can remember of our first encounter," Frank admits, "was how ungodly perky she was for the ungodly hour of five A.M."

Frank Newton Gifford, born on August 16, 1930, in Santa Monica, California, came from an entirely different background from that of Kathie Lee Epstein Johnson. And yet there were similarities in their approach to life. Gifford's father was an oil-drilling superintendent—a typical roughneck spudder during those deep depression days.

However, because he was in the oil business and the oil business was booming in spite of the depression, the Gifford family kept in business all the time, moving from one oil field to another. Mostly the communities were in California—Taft, Watsonville, Stockton, Avenal, Collingo, and Long Beach. In the end they settled down in Bakersfield, named after one of the most famous oil-refining centers.

During Gifford's high school years he found football—or football found him. He was a versatile performer on the team, playing end, quarterback, and halfback positions, excelling at each.

"I wasn't thinking especially about college, because there was no college background in my family." But in his junior year his coach suggested to him that he could go to the University of Southern California if he worked hard enough.

Before attending U.S.C. in 1950, Gifford played two years at Bakersfield Junior College, where he became a triple-threat halfback, leading his team to the Junior Rose Bowl. Then, at the University of Southern California, he became an all-American offensive-defensive back. As the tailback in the team's single-wing offense, he ran, passed, and blocked; as a defensive back, he tackled and defended against passes. In those days players worked in both offense *and* defense positions.

"The tailback has the game to win or lose because so much is expected of him," Gifford once said. "I liked that challenge. I do my best when a lot is expected of me. I loved every second of it."

That was the key to Frank Gifford's character. He loved to be challenged. If a great deal was expected of him, he delivered. With Kathie Lee Epstein, the very same thing was true. She loved to be challenged. She loved to do the impossible. And when it was demanded that she stretch, she stretched even more than the maximum.

Gifford was a shoo-in for the National Football League, where he went to the New York Giants in 1952. Those were great days for the Giants, and for Gifford. He played with them through

1963. In February 1961 he signed a contract as a radio sportscaster for CBS. He also became a scout for the Giants.

In 1951 he had married Maxine Avis Ewart, whom he had met at U.S.C. She was a Phi Beta Kappa and at one time Homecoming Queen at Southern California. They had two boys, Jeffrey and Kyle, and a girl, Victoria. Unfortunately, the marriage did not survive the long years of football and sportscasting. The two of them separated some years later and were divorced.

Gifford liked the challenge of radio, and, as might be expected, he excelled at that, too. His California voice—a kind of no-accent middle-class American amalgam—stood him in good stead on the air. Of course the biggest challenge at that time was television, not radio. But that could wait while Gifford honed his speaking voice for the job he was doing for CBS.

Then in 1970, there was an opening at ABC-TV. When NBC and CBS had divided up the National Football League and the American Football League between them, ABC decided it had to come up with *something* in the matter of competition.

And so *Monday Night Football* was born. Originally the three announcers were Keith Jackson, Howard Cosell, and "Dandy" Don Meredith. Keith Jackson did the play-by-play the first year. But then he left. And it was Frank Gifford, golden boy of the New York Giants (and the Southern California Trojans) who moved into the spot effortlessly and solidified the announcing team.

From the beginning, *Monday Night Football* was a huge success. Men like Fran Tarkenton, Alex Karras, Joe Namath, and O. J. Simpson all served a gig for a year or so. It was the team of Cosell, Meredith, and Gifford that actually made the program into a true viewing event. While Gifford remains to this day, both Cosell and Meredith went on to other things.

Gifford's interest in television was not limited to sports, by any means. And that was the reason he was subbing for David Hartman that morning at ABC-TV when he got his first glimpse of Kathie Lee. Or, rather, when Kathie Lee got her first glimpse of the famous jeans-stretching "tight end."

After seeing Kathie Lee in person, Gifford watched her on *Good Morning America* to see how she looked on the television tube. Actually, he was most unimpressed at what he saw. Kathie Lee was performing her stint on camera, but she was seated in David Hartman's chair. Now Hartman was six feet five inches tall. The chair was cut purposely low for his lengthy torso. That forced Kathie Lee to stretch up as high as she could to read from the TelePrompTer.

Frank was reminded of a turkey craning its neck for a better view of the barnyard. "Albeit," Frank admitted, "it was a very pretty turkey."

Struck by her image, Frank called her up after the show. He did not disguise his reaction to her work. "You look like something eating fruit out of the top of a tree," he told her. The two of them had a good laugh over that, and he exhorted her never to sit in Hartman's chair again. Soon they found out that they had something else very much in common—in addition to their careers in TV. They both had the same birthday—August 16! In spite of their obvious interest in one another their relationship was merely a platonic one for the next four long years.

At the time, Frank was suffering through the disastrous breakdown of a marriage to his second wife, Astrid Lindley, a half-English, half-Norwegian aerobics instructor who was too busy teaching exercises to be with him. The separation became final in 1984.

At this juncture Gifford was so sick of marriage that he told his good friend Don Meredith, the former quarterback of the Dallas Cowboys, to come to his aid if he ever said "I do" again. To wit, if Frank even *thought* about saying those two words, Dandy Don was under direct orders to cut off his—in Frank's words—"what 'I do' it with."

At the time of Frank's separation from his second wife, Kathie Lee was enduring the collapse of her own tenuous marriage to Paul Johnson. Seeing her misery, Frank became a kind of broker for Kathie Lee, supplying her with dates and trying to help her emerge from her charcoal gray emotional funk.

He often felt like an older brother trying to protect a kid sister from the vicissitudes of life, namely, the beasts lurking in the steel and glass jungle of New York City and the backstabbers and professional hitmen climbing to fame in the cutthroat milieu of network television.

In 1986 Frank decided he had just about had it with playing the big brother role to Kathie Lee's kid sister act. He himself was conflicted as to what kind of a career *he* should pursue—whether it was to be as announcer on *Monday Night Football* or as a talk-show host on CBS's morning show. He concluded reluctantly that his role as Kathie Lee's love broker was over.

And so on a warm spring day in 1986, the Giff and Kathie Lee had a friendly lunch at a Mexican restaurant on West Sixty-Ninth Street. Ironically enough, the place was named Santa Fe, "ironically" because that was the name of the famous town in New Mexico in which Frank intended to buy a ranch. The final papers for his divorce from Astrid were only a few weeks away and he wanted to head for the wide open spaces with all possible dispatch as soon as he could.

Kathie Lee was also restless and footloose. She had just walked out on her current boyfriend, after a seething, stormy set-to that was the culmination of a troubled relationship. She was on the downside of a bad fall. Desolated and lonely, she touched Frank in the deepest part of his being.

Later Frank admitted that he had never seen her so drawn. He knew he had to break it off with her. Her troubles seemed to be taking over his whole life. It was not that he wanted out of the friendly relationship they had; it was simply that she seemed to be drowning and pulling him down with her into the vortex.

He decided he was through. "That's *it*," he told her. "You've got to give yourself a break and get off this. You're being hurt too much." And now for the coup de grace. Frank took a deep breath. "Kathie," he said, "from now on, you're hanging out with me."

Luckily Dandy Don was not in town that week. The hanging out began immediately. It was fun. Actually it was also short-lived. The two of them officially tied the knot less than six months later on October 18, 1986, at the beachfront home of one of Frank's prominent attorney friends, Ron Konecky.

Frank recalls the event as an Indian summer day with cool Hamptons breezes and a warm Bakersfield sun shining high in the sky—a combined tribute to his bride's Eastern seacoast upbringing and his own California background.

Everybody came to the wedding, all Giff's pals and their wives, along with Kathie Lee's pals and husbands. Frank was glad his mother had a chance to meet Kathie Lee. She died only a month after the wedding.

Frank had overheard the two of them talking on the phone before the wedding and was pleased to discover that they shared a spiritual bond together, since they were exchanging biblical thoughts and passages with one another.

When *Live With Regis and Kathie Lee* became a hit in the mid-eighties, Frank Gifford became famous as the husband of Kathie Lee. Kathie Lee told her TV audience she wanted Frank to give her a second child after her first, Cody, was born.

After she said that, Frank claimed, "All of a sudden I'm being accosted by a little old Italian woman on the corner of Fifty-Eighth and Park Avenue, yelling, 'Why you no give your wife a bambino?'"

But Frank bears no ill will toward Kathie Lee for revealing all those intimate secrets about their married life. "I never worry about Kathie. I know that she'd never say anything that would embarrass me. She's very aware of how far she can go because she is smart as hell. I've seen people like her in sports. You can see they've got it, and you wonder when things are going to break right for them. When we started going together, things were tough for her. I told her to hang around with me for a while, maybe they would get better."

Even though Kathie Lee has a storybook life, she is just another working stiff, as far as Frank is concerned. "She struggles like any working mother. Everyone wants her time, but Cody and I and now the new baby deserve most of it. She knows that."

"I've had a great life," Frank observed to Mike Lupica in *Esquire* in 1995. "But I haven't had a perfect life. The children from my first marriage, I didn't know them as children. We love each other. But I wasn't here for them. There was football, and then I was so damned busy trying to be somebody in television."

Even though she has a perfect life, Kathie Lee wishes it was even better. She wishes she could spend even more time with Frank and her children.

"I'm always torn," she told the *Ladies Home Journal* in 1993. "I think, Gee, I could be traveling with Frank right now, while he's vital and healthy, or I could have taken my little boy to school this morning. I'm always wondering if I'm making the right choices."

For his part Frank doesn't want Kathie Lee to do too much. "I sometimes get upset with her when she spreads herself too thin. . . . She will never dilute the effort she puts into everything she does. She wants to do everything. And it takes so much out of her, she's absolutely exhausted. It's tough with a baby and trying to keep a home."

Kathie Lee appreciates his concern but doesn't see eye to eye with Frank on this particular subject. "Frank is at the point in his life where he's achieved more than any person could hope to achieve. Trophies don't mean anything to him. He wants me. So if I'm dead set on getting a standing ovation at a concert or winning an Emmy or things that he's already done, then he gets frustrated by the fact that I don't know yet how meaningless those things are.

"But I'm the younger one so I still have things to learn. Sometimes I say, 'Let me experience this.' Even when it came to having a child, he would have preferred that we didn't have one. But he said, 'How can I ask you, who has never had a child, not to have one for my sake?'"

Kathie Lee may discuss intimate details of her marriage in front of a TV audience, but she puts her foot down when it comes to revealing any details about her sex life.

"I won't discuss my sex life with my husband. That's our business. We have double entendres and we allude to things, but my husband's a very private man. That's between us. Otherwise I'd videotape it and show it."

Evidently Frank's foray into the nanny's room while he was stark naked did not count as part of Kathie Lee's sex life with Frank. She told the whole country about that event—to the chagrin of Frank, who objected to the disclosure.

Here is Frank's interpretation of what *really* happened that night:

"Our bedroom, Cody's bedroom, and the bedroom of his nanny—Christine Gardner—all adjoin." The Giffords had hired Christine shortly before Cody's birth. She had become part of the Gifford retinue. When Cody was still a small child, Frank awoke in the middle of the night one time. Half-asleep and without a stitch of clothes on, he wandered in to check on his son.

"He was fine, so I went to the bathroom down the hall, and, on the way back, noticed a door open. I peeked in, and there was our dog, Chablis, curled up at the foot of a bed."

Chabby usually slept with the Giffords. Frank went into the room and sat on the edge of the bed, where he began absently petting his dog. Then, quite suddenly, he became aware that he and Chabby were not alone.

"Frank?" said a very concerned Christine Gardner.

Frank realized instantly what had happened. In a shot he bolted up, ran back to the master bedroom, and jumped into bed with Kathie Lee. Finally, overcome with embarrassment, he worked up enough nerve to jostle her awake and tell her the whole weird story.

And lived to regret it.

"Big mistake. The next morning the viewers of *Live With Regis and Kathie Lee* learned from Mrs. Frank Gifford that Mr. Frank Gifford had sleepwalked naked into the nanny's bedroom. The next thing I knew, the supermarket tabloids jumped on the story—only now it's KATHIE LEE'S HUBBY IN BED WITH NANNY! Needless to say, that story's haunted me ever since."

Kathie Lee's revelation of Frank's contretemps to the entire country reinforced his first impression of her, which was pretty much the same thing everyone else thought about her. "You've got to quiet this woman down. She [is] a lot of fun, but that early in the morning it's kind of tough."

Frank knew that most people who didn't know her found it hard to believe that she was simply a very honest person. In the sophisticated world of communications, people were prone to be a little more inhibited about personal things; at least they didn't blurt out every detailed thought in their heads. But those who knew Kathie Lee all loved her. It took them a while to realize that what you saw in Kathie Lee was the real thing.

Frank pointed out, "Ever since *Live With Regis and Kathie Lee* became the talk of television, people constantly ask me the same question: Is the woman I'm married to anything like the woman they see on the screen? Not just *anything* like her, I always reply—she's totally like her. What you see is what she is."

Frank has nothing but praise for Kathie Lee. "For openers, Kathie's intelligence is off the charts. I mean, nobody I know is smarter or quicker. She also doesn't hide anything: Everything that emanates from her mouth is totally honest."

Frank believes that Kathie Lee's honesty and straightforwardness gets her in trouble too much of the time. But while she sometimes gets hit hard by enemies who envy her, she is a person who wouldn't hurt a soul. "She wouldn't hurt an enemy if she had one," Frank avows.

For his money, Kathie Lee's overpowering ambition is not fueled by her greed for power, for success, or for fabulous wealth. "Believe me, it's not ego. She's just an extremely talented person

145

who, I think, feels that God intended her to maximize those talents.

"And once she gets involved with a project, it's always 190 percent. Sometimes she gets so caught up in it, so enthusiastic, that I can just see her little motor overheating. So I'll put my arm around her and turn off my imaginary switch on her shoulder—sort of like shutting down a windup doll."

She doesn't like that. "Don't you do that to me," she'll say to Frank. But sometimes he slows her down just a bit anyway. Other times he doesn't, but at least she knows what he's thinking.

Frank just wishes Kathie Lee would relax once in a while and sniff the flowers. "We try to accommodate each other. But right now she's doing far more than I would like her to do. Frankly, we don't need the money. I try hard not to make it difficult for her, but sometimes it's tough for me not to say, 'Knock that crap off. You don't need it!'"

Frank understands why Kathie Lee pushes herself so hard and he can empathize with her desire to accomplish even more. She never got anything the easy way. She had to work hard for every little thing she got. She did all the scut work when she was on the way up, absorbed all the rejections, and underwent all the harassment that good-looking women are subject to before she finally made it to the top.

And all the more power to her, he thought, for sticking to it and trying all the time, in spite of all the obstacles and pitfalls in her way.

The Giff knows how hard it is for her to turn down a golden opportunity today, now that she had made it. In fact, it's *doubly* difficult to refuse a good offer. Even though he wants her to take it easy more, he doesn't blame her in the least for working harder than ever. It is simply in her character always to try to excel. And good for her to keep on trying!

Kathie Lee has explained that her inability to say no to anyone stems from her youth, where she craved approval. "I've always been very approval-oriented," she has said. "When I was little,

I'd make cookies so people in the neighborhood would like me. If a grouchy neighbor said, 'Don't cross my grass,' I'd say, 'I'm going to bake her a cake.'"

Regarding her personal life, she says, "It really didn't come together for me until Frank. He just plain loved me unconditionally. I loved him in the same way. It was a healing for both of us."

For Frank, his meeting Kathie Lee changed his life too. "She made me laugh all the time. She was hysterical." That was the reason he fell in love with her.

Kathie Lee can't help it if Frank doesn't like her whirlwind of activity at times. That's just the way she is, like it or lump it.

As she told *Good Housekeeping* in May 1994, "There are days when he's great about it, and other days when it just frustrates him to pieces." She knows very well that there are times when the Giff feels neglected; she knows he has a right to feel that way. It's just the way things are. And, by the same token, Kathie Lee feels kind of neglected during football season when the Giff is out every Monday night as part of the *Monday Night Football* team for ABC-TV.

The relationship is saved by a strong and growing friendship between the two—something not quite like love, but similar and as strong a tie. They do love one another, and also have a tremendous respect for each other's work. "That's what gets us through times like that," Kathie Lee says.

She still remembers how Frank surprised her for her fortieth birthday, showing full well that he wasn't neglecting her at all.

As Kathie Lee recalls it, the Giffords were going to Colorado on vacation. She was fighting a losing battle with the washing machine and its load of curtains and diapers. And then, just before they left, Frank gave Kathie Lee a surprise birthday party in their New York apartment.

He had the big lie all fashioned. The idea was that the Disney people were in town and Kathie Lee was to meet with them before the Giffords left for Colorado. Kathie Lee dutifully got Cody and

Cassidy into the city, under the impression, created by the Giff, that this was going to be a little dinner at the Gifford apartment. She walked in the door unsuspecting, and saw that there were about a hundred people there.

But that wasn't the worst of it.

Kathie Lee was totally unprepared. She was wearing her nursing bra. It had been very uncomfortable in the car driving down to the city. Before going in to meet her guests, she took a quick detour into a private vestibule where she started fiddling with the bra to make it more comfortable.

"I walked in and there's Regis, and I'm standing with my hand in my bra trying to fix it. Only *I* would have a situation like that."

"Surprise!" the hundred-odd guests cried out.

And Kathie Lee had the last word. "You're not *kidding*!"

Everything is fine as long as no one tries to flirt with Frank at a party. Then Kathie Lee can fly off the handle.

Frank once recalled an incident that occasioned total rage in Kathie Lee: "It was the time we attended Kathie's first Kentucky Derby. The night before the race we went to a huge cocktail party in an old Louisville hotel."

As they left the party on their way to dinner, Frank headed for the men's room and Kathie Lee for the ladies' room. As Frank stood at the urinal, he heard a female voice asking the attendant outside, "Was that Frank Gifford who just went into the men's room?"

Seconds later—surprise! The woman was inside the john with him! She sat down on the washbasin.

"I've always wanted to meet you, Frank." Frank couldn't help but wave away the fumes of mint julep that wafted out of her mouth.

The story didn't end there.

"I certainly wasn't going to let her chase me out of the men's room," Frank said.

When they left together, their departure coincided with Kathie Lee's return from the ladies' room. Frank saw the fire in Kathie

Lee's eyes. "I knew my newfound friend was in deep trouble," he added.

Kathie Lee let it all come out. *"What the hell are you doing with my husband?"* she screamed. There followed one of the greatest disappearing acts in history. Miss Mint Julep simply *vanished*.

"I mean," Frank said, "she moved faster than Secretariat."

Kathie Lee was glaring at Frank, as if somehow *he* had caused it all. Luckily, there was no one else was around.

"Imagine what the *National Enquirer* would have made of *that!*" Frank sighed.

When the Giffords had their son, Cody, Frank's life changed. According to Frank, their first child was conceived on a five-day cruise along the Italian Riviera. The newly married Giffords were spending their time on one of Carnival's four-masted sailing ships for their honeymoon. Cody Newton Gifford came into the world on March 22, 1990—and the Giff's world was suddenly filled with what he called "a whole lot of joy."

There's even a story behind the name Cody, too. Typically, the Giffords got the baby's name from a football telecast. Here's how it happened. It was Thanksgiving, and Frank was sitting in his in-laws' home in Bowie, Maryland, watching the Cleveland Browns play the Detroit Lions. He and Kathie Lee had known for some time that the baby would be a boy, and they were still arguing about what to name him.

Frank was watching the television screen, and an offensive tackle for the Browns made a big play. The Browns player was Cody Risien, an old friend of Frank's.

"Hey, what about 'Cody'?" Frank called out to Kathie Lee in the kitchen.

"Cody," she said, sort of rolling the name around on her tongue. "Hey," she said, "I think I love it. I *do* love it. That's it!" It didn't take long for her active mind to add a middle name to Cody. "Cody Newton!" she cried out enthusiastically—Newton being, of course, Frank's own middle name.

"Cody Newton Gifford . . . Cody Newton Gifford. . . ."

The Giffords soon decided they wanted another child after having Cody. Kathie Lee was the first to decide in favor of having a second baby. She then had to persuade Frank that it was the right thing to do. Frank hesitated at first. After all, he already had children from a previous marriage, and also grandchildren.

According to Frank in his autobiography, *The Whole Nine Yards*, Kathie Lee took the issue to the air waves, telling her TV audience that Frank didn't want another child. She thought this might help persuade him to change his mind. It did. In fact, it led to the scene on Fifty-Eighth and Park Avenue, where an Italian woman accused him of denying Kathie Lee her most sacred wish.

Frank maintained all along that he never really needed any convincing. He had always wanted another child, not for his sake, but for Cody's. He wanted Cody to know what it was like to have a little brother or sister.

It looked like the Giffords were going to have another child in July 1992, but that wasn't meant to be.

Frank has vivid memories of the fateful weeks that followed Kathie Lee's discovery that she was pregnant for the second time. That was in July 1992. The Giffords needed a vacation badly, and Frank and Kathie Lee flew to Vail, Colorado, where they have a house. Kathie Lee was exhausted from fighting a very lingering head cold. She couldn't use any medications, which, of course, are prohibitive for a pregnant woman.

It was on a gloomy, rainy Friday that she began having trouble. Finally, late Saturday afternoon Frank heard her run for the bathroom.

"I heard a loud moan," Frank recalls.

He ran in just as she began to sob distractedly. He knew what had happened. She had miscarried. And she was totally inconsolable.

The tragedy was not enough to make the Giffords forsake their dream of having a sister or brother for little Cody. In fact, that very same year, this time in November, and, ironically enough, also in Vail, it happened again, and Kathie Lee conceived for the third time.

Frank pointed out, "We also settled on the name of Cassidy, a name we not only both liked but one that would fit either a boy or a girl."

A month after they had decided on "Cassidy" Frank got a Christmas card from Cody Risien—Cody's namesake. They had begun writing letters back and forth.

This card told the story briefly. The Risiens had had a baby daughter. And her name was—Cassidy!

"Oh, my God," Frank thought. "Cody Risien is going to think something's really weird." Then he shrugged. "As a matter of fact, now that I think about it, my life really isn't a beautiful play. I'm actually living inside a beautiful sitcom—and there's only one name for it: *I Love Kathie.*"

13

Regis as Comedian:
The World According to Reege

A cclaim for Regis Philbin is unanimous and ubiquitous among his comedian peers.

"He's just about the best there is at what he does," said David Letterman recently. "It must be odd to be his age and be at the top of your game. He just wears me out."

Fellow comedian Dana Carvey, of *Saturday Night Live* fame, and several-times guest cohost of *Live With Regis and Kathie Lee*, almost gushes with admiration for Philbin.

"Regis embodies comedy in the classic form. He's the Put-Upon Guy, the guy who always gets the bad seat at the roast and isn't afraid to tell you about it. He has no pretenses. He's totally honest on the air, and if you're totally honest, how are you not cool?"

Even Arsenio Hall has said, "You ain't hip unless you watch Regis and Kathie Lee."

Jerry Seinfeld, another peer in the field of comedy, only has praise for Philbin and Kathie Lee Gifford. "I, for one, couldn't be more impressed. You can't do less than they do and make a living."

Philbin's cohost Kathie Lee Gifford adores Philbin. She has never met another performer who is as comfortable as Regis is in a live, improvisational situation. Most performers—especially actors and actresses—are very uneasy without a script. They are used to having their words crafted for them by someone else.

As Kathie Lee sees it, Regis himself *is* a character already. No one needs to write what he says to make him into Regis Philbin. He has created himself and knows exactly what to do to be himself. And "Reege" knows a lot about the psychology of performing, too. Performers are usually reluctant to talk about their real complaints in front of other people. They keep them bottled up inside.

But both Regis and Kathie Lee know that sometimes it is a delight for an audience to hear what inner ills are bothering a performer—the more famous the better. Both she and Regis have made a career out of complaining, themselves. Their complaints are adroit and nicely worded. They come out real, even if they are thought up and articulated on the spur of the moment.

In turn, Regis's quirky personality is just a bit ill at ease about his newfound success. He resents it, in a way. He knows it has little to do with his work or his skills at being a talk-show host. He knows it's just the way show business operates. A long drought—then sudden, dazzling success!

In his long wait for that elevator to take him to the top of his profession, Regis had seen exactly the same thing happen to actors, to actresses, to singers, and all kinds of other performers. Success has a snowball effect. The more publicity a rising star gets, the bigger he—or she—gets. And the bigger he or she becomes.

The thing that Regis never forgets is that he is doing exactly the same show that he started with way back in San Diego—and now suddenly his ratings are going up. He and Kathie Lee are no better, nor are they any worse. They just happen to be on a roll now.

Like Kathie Lee—who believes in laughing at herself before someone else does—Regis too feels that he can kid himself all the time, and make people like it. Apparently the public agrees with him.

Weeks before they hosted their first Miss America Pageant in 1991, Regis said, "Our humor can be acerbic. Why do I want to inflict myself on this institution?" He added, "I look cross-eyed at Miss Arkansas and the whole thing goes boom."

"I just want you to be you," answered Kathie Lee. "Just direct all your acerbic thrusts in my direction."

Philbin wanted to introduce some excitement into what he considered to be a staid pageant—one that could stand just a little bit of loosening up. He was tired of hearing everyone good-mouthing everyone else until it sounded like treacle time.

One innovation was a "gab session" à la Regis and Kathie Lee—exactly like the first seventeen minutes of the host chat that opens each *Live* show. Then the five panelists—judges—would join Regis and Kathie Lee on the stage, and be interviewed about the judging of the beauty contestants.

And, along with bringing some comedy and some talk to the pageant, Philbin and Kathie Lee would also sing. Together they would perform the famous "There She Goes" coronation song.

And, as if that wasn't quite enough, they would soft-pedal the bathing suit portion of the contest, knowing that women's liberationists now looked askance at it and considered it to be one of their primary targets—exploitation of the female form.

Regis turned serious. "This sounds like a joke," he said, "but personality is the first thing I notice in a woman."

The programming seemed quite tight and balanced. Yet Philbin wouldn't have minded at all if the production of the show turned out to be flawed in some way.

"We kind of enjoy it when things go wrong. We've been through every mishap you can imagine on television. We wouldn't mind if that happened. That would be great."

During the event, everything went smoothly, there were laughs where they should have been, and the Miss America Pageant came off very well.

"If I don't win Miss Congeniality, then the thing is fixed!" Philbin had said just before the curtain went up.

He didn't actually win anything. Except the knowledge that he had updated the rather traditional precepts of the Miss America Pageant.

Though he may not understand it, Regis Philbin basks in his late-blooming fame. It's a far cry from his early days.

Now, even the picky Madonna can be included among his fans. She likes *Regis and Kathie Lee* so much she called them up asking to appear on it. During the show on which she guested, Regis said to her, "Tell me the truth. Am I an attractive man or not?" She answered yes.

Supermodel Cindy Crawford likes to feel Philbin's biceps and take workouts with him at a local New York gym. She once confided a secret to a reporter about Regis: "He likes to look at himself in the mirror while he does those biceps curls."

TV critic Tom Shales thinks Philbin is ne plus ultra. He even gave this advice to aspiring comedian Conan O'Brien: He said, "Watch Regis to understand Philbin's ability to make entertainment out of nothing, to bound onto the air day after day, always personable and amusing."

For Shales's money, "They [Regis and Kathie Lee] can be flirtatious and as long as it's not consummated it generates a pleasant suspense. It gives what seems an edgeless show an edge. It's fun to watch them fight and make up."

Of course Philbin flirts outrageously with guests as well as with Kathie Lee. For instance, he interviewed Madonnna on the sixteenth floor of the Four Seasons Hotel in Los Angeles, where she showed up in nothing more than a flimsy nightgown. After the interview Philbin said on his show, "I would say she kind of liked me. You could see a little bit of animal magnetism."

The entertainment columnist for the *Los Angeles Daily News* put in his oar, too. "For all their quirks, for all their annoying qualities, there's something comfortable about [Regis and Kathie Lee]. I personally don't want to hear more about Cody [Gifford], but it's like a soap opera—you begin to care whether Cody is throwing up on Frank. You watch them a little bit every day, and they become a part of your life."

When Jerry Seinfeld claimed that Philbin did nothing on the *Regis and Kathie Lee* show, Regis resented it. "What we do is very deceptive. I don't know if Jerry Seinfeld or anybody else could do what we do every day."

Kathie Lee agreed. "It ain't easy being easy," she said in the immortal words of Don Meredith—quondam Dallas Cowboys quarterback and easygoing ex-football announcer for *Monday Night Football* and a personal friend, through her husband Frank.

David Letterman likes Philbin so much he calls him "Show Saver" and frequently invites him onto the Letterman show. On one such occasion, Philbin stood behind the curtains preparing to walk onstage, listening to Letterman and informing a reporter what was going on in front of the curtain.

"Listen," said Philbin. "The audience is dying down! [Letterman] always does two bits too many. . . . Show Saver's gonna have to gear up! Gonna have to get out there and win one for Dave! . . . He's beginning to flounder. . . . Dave's voice is getting higher! Panic is setting in! I've been there. I know—"

At that moment Letterman announced, "And *finally*—oh boy, and not a minute too soon—finally. . . ."

Hearing his cue, Regis Philbin charged onto the stage, the Seventh Cavalry to the rescue.

Kathie Lee has explained the charm of their show in this manner: "Regis and I come out every day unscripted, unrehearsed. And we have fun. It's a very simple thing. Fun is contagious."

Her cohost couldn't agree more. "It's a whole mood that's conducive to 'Let's see what they're going to be talking about today; let's see what happened to them last night.'"

And why shouldn't he agree? He's the one who invented the "host chat" concept for the show.

He feels that Kathie Lee fits hand in glove with the show and that it is primarily her exuberance that is a perfect foil for his irascible gibes.

As he told the *Hartford Courant* in 1992, "She's an ebullient, overwhelming type of personality. There's no intrigue. There's no problem here. I think she's terrific.

"I feel like I can have a rapport and make chemistry—I hate that word, but that's the word—with anyone, and I have.

"But Kathie is a special person. Very show business savvy. And she knew right from the beginning what I was all about, what the [show's] opening was all about—it was a freefall exchange, and it had to be fresh, and she fell right into it. Right from the beginning I knew she was going to be great." And he was so right.

Philbin could see that his show was taking off when *Saturday Night Live* started satirizing it. Dana Carvey played Philbin as a harried man outraged by the merest slight. For one skit Carvey ranted about attending a charity ball and "sittin' down with the wife at our reserved table, because I'm such a big *star*, and we're behind the *pole*—we can't . . . see . . . *the band*!"

Philbin loved the spoof. "Wasn't that a scream? It's supposed to be an exaggeration. The more I listen to that tape the more I begin to sound like that. It's beginning to *disturb* me."

He finds it tough sledding, competing against his fellow talk-show hosts. "See, Geraldo's talking about the devil. Joan has got a pimp. Sally had a mother-daughter stripper team. You can't compete with sleaze like that. I'm fighting for my *life*!"

To hear Phil tell it, the year 1988 was one of the roughest periods for *Live With Regis and Kathie Lee*. "That was the year that Oprah lost fifty pounds, Phil wore a dress, Geraldo broke his nose. Nobody noticed *Regis and Kathie Lee*."

But that was nothing compared to the debacle known as the *Joey Bishop* show, whose nightmarish memory Philbin can't quite shake even to this day.

Philbin is not afraid to voice his opinions of comedians. About Johnny Carson's retirement, he said at the time, "I think he's going nuts right now. The closer it got to the end, the less he wanted to go."

And "I love Letterman but don't see him often, since he goes on too late."

As for Dennis Miller, "I sympathize with him. I know what it's like to start a new show."

Regarding Arsenio Hall: "Just a phenomenon. That opening with flashing lights—the best ever."

Not to be left out, Jay Leno elicited these comments: "His monologues were the sharpest political commentary ever. He seems to have eased up. But he's got tremendous empathy with kids."

Concerning his son Danny, Regis told *Esquire* in 1994, "He's my hero in life. For him to overcome all this disability, to graduate from college, work on his master's program—he's just dynamite, a remarkable kid. Now he's got a permanent job coming up. But it's been a *grind*. I remember for one year straight he was in the hospital, and I'd go see him every day. I'll tell you, anytime he goes back into the hospital, it's like a knife in my heart. I wish it were me, not him."

Regis Philbin will never hit below the belt in his comedy the way a Howard Stern does, even though he has admitted, "Sometimes we [Kathie Lee and he] do get carried away. I'm just afraid to say, 'Let's never say that again.' You see, we've never really put any restraints on ourselves because once you do that, you're going to chip away at that little special fifteen, twenty minutes there, and if we have to put our kid gloves on and worry about everybody's feelings, it's gonna get screwed up."

On one show, Kathie Lee asked Regis about that repulsive festering thing on Philbin's cheek.

"I don't want to talk about this!" yelled Philbin, put out that she would broach the subject of the cancer on his face. "But the mouth had to bring it up!"

Michael Gelman considers Philbin and Kathie Lee's relationship as "friendly, and it's businesslike, and they're very close, but they really lead separate lives."

Kathie Lee can't think of another cohost she would rather work with than Regis Philbin. "I have been through this man's kidney stones. He has been through my pregnancy and my bloated belly and my sore nipples. We have been through ear hairs together. I pluck 'em for him sometimes. . . . I think I was the first person Regis worked with who had as much experience as he did, so I think he had a lot of respect for me."

Sometimes Regis thinks he owes his success simply to durability. "You know what I think it is. I think if you hang around long enough, they go through everybody else, and eventually they get around to you. . . . It gets to be your fifteen minutes."

Kathie Lee has her own idea why the show is topping the charts. "Regis and I do not mind looking stupid or ugly."

As simple as that.

The price of success: the dreaded tabloids.

After reading one in November 1990 Kathie Lee asked Regis, "Do you know what I was doing last week, Reege? I was having secret meetings at NBC headquarters because I'm taking over Deborah Norville's job—as if I'd leave you for Bryant Gumble!"

"It's really incredible, isn't it," he replied, bridling.

"Critics are constantly saying everybody copies everybody else; where are the fresh ideas? Where is something new? Something different? We think we do something completely different and very dangerous and something a lot of people don't have the courage to try every day, which is totally live, unscripted television.

"We thought of all people the television critics would say, 'Hey look, this may not be your cup of tea, but at least give credit where credit is due.'"

"Not one word," said Regis Philbin, miffed. "We've been national for two years, and not one word of grudging recognition for what we're doing."

People were too busy watching those other guys who have talk shows.

Philbin pointed out, "Some mornings Geraldo will have five lesbians and Sally [Jessy Raphael] will have five grandfathers who want to dress like grandmothers and we're doing household chores. People say, how are we going to get a rating? Well, the funny thing is, people are beginning to recognize the difference between what we're doing and what they're doing."

He went on. "Whatever happens to us becomes part of our show. We don't have any writers and we have to use real-life things."

Like the time Kathie Lee attended a party given by the Irish Chamber of Commerce honoring Regis Philbin. She mentioned Philbin's wife Joy and related this little irreverent story about her:

"Joy had one critical moment there, after all the Irish people finished giving their speeches and all the ladies at the Waldorf Astoria went to the bathroom. There must have been a line of fifteen women, and Joy was standing there going—"

Instead of using words, Kathie Lee choreographed what happened by dancing a jig like a kid does when nature calls.

Regis shook his head in disgust at her. And the audience cracked up, loving every minute of it.

It was a typical example of their off-the-cuff comedy, and all of it took place live in New York, without even the standard seven-second tape delay used to censor other supposedly live shows.

Another one of their comedic exchanges went like this in 1993:

"*I have heard you snore!*" Philbin told Kathie Lee.

"You *what?*"

"*I have slept with you!*"

The color drained from Kathie Lee's face, until she realized what he was talking about. Then she relaxed.

"He's technically right," she told the studio audience. "On planes." Wanting to get even with him, she retorted with her own zinger. "Do you know what I do when you're sleeping?" she asked him. "I dab your drool!"

Asked about their sharp verbal exchanges, Regis told the *Washington Post* that Kathie Lee "does get on my nerves once in a while, as I do hers. But what I hate are the hosts who are too civil, too nice to one another. I like to keep an edge between us.

And if it looks like there's an antagonistic thing, well, maybe there is."

The feeling is mutual.

"I could never be married to Regis," Kathie Lee told the same newspaper. "My gosh, we'd kill each other! Actually, I'd kill him. I'd win."

In fact, Kathie Lee would like to crown Philbin at least once "every day." This despite the fact that "there is a great affection between us. Great affection and great respect."

For the show, Philbin likes to recount humiliating events that happen to him. After all, a king should not have to suffer any degradation. On a 1991 episode Regis made the mistake of tripping on a cobblestone. He milked the following routine out of it, which doesn't read very funny, but which he and Kathie Lee made funny simply by the way they executed it.

> PHILBIN: I could feel myself spinning *out of control!*
> KATHIE LEE: Reege!
> PHILBIN: Usually I'm agile and I can handle it.
> KATHIE LEE: Reege!
> PHILBIN: There are hundreds of people looking. One guy said, "Oh, that's that Regis Philbin!"

Kathie Lee's screaming out of "Reege!" live comes across as funny. Some call it chemistry, but whatever it is, their interactions are humorous and crack up over eighteen million fans weekly.

As far as Kathie Lee is concerned, "We're the two most uncool people in the world. . . . Regis and I bring out the naughtiness in each other."

When Philbin says something she considers distasteful on the show, she calls it an "oinker," or she may scream, "Outregis!"

As Dana Carvey well knows, and he makes use of it in his impersonation of Regis, one of the host's favorite expressions on the show is *"Are you ready for this?"*

Philbin is also fond of using nicknames as part of his routine.

Anyone who regularly watches his show knows that "Love-ya-baby, Love-ya-baby" is his agent. "The Winds of War" is his sister-in-law. "Steve I Don't Need the Money" is his contractor. "Radu the Killer Whale" is his gym trainer. And "Gelman" is Michael Gelman, his thirtyish, long-haired, ponytailed executive producer whom Regis blames for every mishap the show suffers as Gelman stands patiently by offstage watching things fall apart.

Of course, the truth of the matter is that Gelman too welcomes blunders on the program. "The old adage about never booking kids or animals?" Gelman observes wryly. "I go the total opposite. I love to book kids and animals because there's so much that can go wrong. And when those things go wrong, you have some of the funniest moments of live TV."

In this respect Philbin is somewhat like Johnny Carson in that he seems funnier when his material bombs. The only difference is that Carson worked from a script, while Philbin wings everything from the word go.

Regis's idol nowadays is Don Rickles in lieu of Jack Paar, though Philbin doesn't get as nasty as Rickles. Philbin is always carping about how rotten everything is in the life of the king—himself—as Kathie Lee cries, "Oh, Reege!" in sympathy or in maternal rebuke.

No wonder David Letterman, Barbara Bush, Hillary Rodham Clinton, Donald Trump, and millions of others watch *Live With Regis and Kathie Lee*. In fact, Trump first publicized his proposal to Marla Maples over the phone on the show. Ed McMahon also announced his most recent marriage on *Regis and Kathie Lee*, in person yet.

Kathie Lee is overjoyed that Regis has succeeded at last on TV after so many years of struggle. "I'm happier in a way for Reege than for myself. Because he sort of pioneered the whole thing, that whole fifteen-minute 'host chat' thing.

"And I came in on it and just sort of fit in. But he pioneered it. He's the one that national success has eluded for all these years, and he deserves it. That he's finally getting his due after thirty years, I mean, it makes you happy for him."

With that history behind him, Regis Philbin even now doesn't feel secure in his success. "You keep looking over your shoulder for the next calamity to catch up with you."

14

Kathie Lee as Entertainer:

The World According to Kathie Lee

Unlike the acclaim for Regis Philbin that is unanimous and ubiquitous among his peers, acclaim for Kathie Lee Gifford has never been and never will be an instantaneous and pervasive thing. Yet it is not quite cricket to call her unpopular. She *is* popular. People buy tickets to hear her singing concerts. People pay millions to buy her recordings and tapes.

And people tune in every day to listen to her bicker with Regis "Put-Upon" Philbin.

Hers is a perfect example of a conflicted image. Unlike most people in show business, Kathie Lee never opted for a specific facade that would be her bellwether and would draw people to her. Actually, she developed over the years—and the development tended to be lumpy, without direction, and sometimes off-putting, to say the least.

She came up the hard way, and it was at her own choice. The

easy way would have been to slip into the well-worn, well-received, and well-revered accoutrements of the typical sophisticated performer. In that way, she could have hidden the spots that seemed to make her less than desirable to the average city-bred and "with it" talk fan of the era.

It was the permissive sixties that nurtured her. And yet she chose to be on the other side of the fence from the typical show biz personality—the entertainer at Woodstock, the amplified guitar player of the "folk song" set, the anti-Establishment wisecracker of those wide-open, in-your-face years.

She selected gospel music to sing because she considered herself a born-again Christian. That particular distinction was almost unheard of in the halls of sixties entertainment. Others sang of the winds that were a-blowin'. Kathie Lee sang of God.

She tended to be an embarrassment to people who were "in the know" and "sociologically chic."

It was a time for all kinds of experimentation—the single mother being one of the most widespread statements of feminism in those years. Kathie Lee, on the other hand, chose to remain a virgin until she was married. Unheard of!

These elements of her character were not popular with the public. In her early years she had to overcome the distaste of many of her colleagues—and of those who hired her for public performance. It was not an easy thing to be Kathie Lee Epstein the gospel singer.

Incredibly, Kathie Lee believed that she would grow up to be a better woman if she always told the truth—or at least dealt with truth rather than with its opposite. She was the exact mirror image of sophistication. She was honest and based her actions on her own integrity.

This in itself was unusual enough to make her an anomaly along her peers in show business.

In 1992, Kathie Lee, then thirty-nine years old, published her autobiography *Kathie Lee Gifford: I Can't Believe I Said That!* It was written with the help of coauthor Jim Jerome. Because Kathie Lee was known for her cohost spot on the *Regis and Kathie Lee* show, the book became a quick bestseller with many reviews.

Lauri Githens reviewed the book for the *Buffalo News*. Her findings reveal much about the prevalent taste of the American reader:

"Before the first two pages of this book are over, Kathie Lee Gifford has mentioned her husband, Frank, seven times." She goes on to say that the reader is going to have to *like* Frank Gifford a great deal to get through the book. But, she adds, the reader has to like Kathie Lee Gifford a great deal, too. "And I mean, *really* like her," Githens stresses.

Kathie Lee is characterized as "diverse, blunt, often coarse, and yet touchingly and utterly devoted to her husband and son, Cody." Githens also lauds her for her candid appraisal of great people, as when she "rips into the Queen of England for dressing like an upper-class bag lady."

But candor can be a downer, too. "Jeez, Kath," she writes, "do we really need to know about that Arkansas-sized zit you had when you went to the White House? Or what your thighs look like out of support hose? Or just how virginal you were on your wedding day, and what a crushing disappointment your wedding night was?"

In fact she focuses on Kathie Lee's "very long attempt to explain the heartbreak of her first marriage in 1976 to gospel composer Paul Johnson," concentrating on their "really, really horrible sex life."

The review ends: "Well. Say what you want about Kathie Lee Gifford—because God knows she'll say just about anything she wants, about whomever she has a mind to discuss—you can't read this book cover to cover and knock the woman for being just another media phony. Because she's not; she is the genuine ticket: the sassy girl-next-door who grew up, lost a few dreams and years along the way, hung on to her faith and herself, and made good in the end."

Katy Kelly didn't really *review* the book for *USA Today*, she simply chatted about it—but she does reveal an interesting bias. Her first words are a quotation from Kathie Lee: "I'm fully aware that there are people out there who look at me and want to throw up."

Kelly quotes Kathie Lee about her ex-husband, Paul Johnson. "It's got to be hard for him," Kathie Lee says, referring to her own present superstardom. "He has to look at images of me bombarding him every day, my commercials, my show. . . . When the tabloids came out with that ugly article that said he was gay, it was a flat-out lie."

She and her ex are still friends, she said, and he was consulted by her while the book was being written. "My biggest concern was that I be kind to him," Kathie Lee said. "I asked [Paul] to help us write the book . . . so that it would be done fairly. I didn't want to write this book to cause pain in anybody's life. If I was going to badmouth my ex-husband I would have done it eleven years ago when he walked out on me, when I was really hurt."

The reviewer makes no judgments on the writing itself, or the structure of the book, but simply runs over the parts that interest her.

On the other hand, Diane White of the *Boston Globe* gave an incisive critique of the book as follows:

"As showbiz biography, *I Can't Believe I Said That!* is unusual in that the author doesn't provide a list of men she had affairs with but rather a list of men she could have had affairs with, but didn't. She's a little slippery about the juicy details of her pre-Frank Gifford romantic life: 'It was two years of a hectic life-style. . . .' Tell us more. Kathie Lee! But she doesn't. And she's something less than totally forthcoming about her first marriage to Christian composer Paul Johnson, so the reader is left wondering what, exactly, went on—or didn't go on—between the two of them."

Parts of Kathie Lee's book were excerpted in several women's magazines, each one selecting a different part of the book for reprint, or selectively rewriting sections for publication. After *People* magazine had printed a condensed and reworked excerpt, letters began coming into the editorial offices of the magazine. One was from Paul Johnson, Kathie Lee's ex-husband. He was miffed at the treatment of his marriage in the book *and* the magazine.

"I have much different memories of my wedding night with Kathie Lee," he began. "The honeymoon pictures I have show both of us to be happy and playful and very much in love. Everything about it was 'successful' for me. This is the first time I've heard that it wasn't for her.

"In spinning this yarn to have a best-selling book, Kathie Lee has documented to the world the very reason why our marriage failed. It's impossible to build genuine intimacy with someone who converts every private and sacred moment into burlesque material for her public forum."

To corroborate Johnson's response, Roy M. Carlisle, a friend of Johnson and Kathie Lee, wrote the following letter to *People*:

"Kathie Lee Gifford has turned her need to rewrite history into a Judas-like fine art. I have known Paul Johnson, her first husband, like a brother for over twenty-four years, and I listened to his pain during the marriage and the divorce.

"We who were there know that Kathie Lee's version of the story will please her fans."

Other readers who had never known either of the people concerned also felt that she had made too much of the divorce.

For example, Elizabeth White wrote:

"I have long thought Kathie Lee Gifford was brain-dead, and your article confirms my suspicions. How dare she call an amicable divorce and one miscarriage 'suffering'! Perhaps Kathie Lee, Frank, and that spoiled child of theirs should skip Colorado and take their next vacation some place they've never been before— reality."

Nor were others particularly excited about what the book revealed.

From Myra Weaver to *People*: "Kathie Lee Gifford grew up comfortably, with career breaks beyond what her limited talents deserve. She has a great husband, a healthy son, a gorgeous home and a life filled with vacations and parties. Her failed marriage was a simple matter of incompatibility, and a miscarriage is unfortunately not uncommon. Nor is it life threatening."

On the other hand, some were appreciative of the story and the book:

Karen Leanne Hamel wrote: "What a lovely, charming article. I watch *Live With Regis and Kathie Lee* faithfully every morning because of her upbeat, cheery personality. It's nice to know that it's not just an act and that she is truly happy. She deserves whatever good things might come her way!"

And Jeannine Ahlberg Glenn wrote: "As an avid fan of Kathie Lee Gifford, I want to thank you for the fantastic article and pictures. Kathie Lee is clearly a role model and inspiration to marriage and motherhood, but shame on you for putting Madonna on the same cover."

The Kathie Lee Gifford personality, long on the candid and short on the reserved, occasionally reaped numbers of negativistic stories in newspapers and magazines—particularly after her autobiography had been printed and remained a bestseller for three months in 1992 and 1993.

A journalist named Sarah Tippit was assigned to cover a press conference in Orlando, Florida, by the *Orlando Sentinel Tribune* in January 1994. The occasion was a celebration of Kathie Lee's new line of clothing, called "Kathie Lee for Plaza South," manufactured by Halmode. The affair was held at Dillards in Orlando's Florida Mall.

Tippit begins her story with a brief rundown of Kathie Lee's successes in gospel singing and television, and then gets down to business. A fashion show has preceded Kathie Lee's arrival, and the star then shows up "in a whirl of white: white limo, white outfit, white anecdote." Tippit writes that "Gifford," as she calls Kathie Lee, explains she has been rehearsing for a Disney Christmas show when she suddenly begins choking on a cloud of fake snow.

Tippit, quoting Kathie Lee: "'I walk out all dressed to kill in my Kathie Lee for Plaza South, and this blast of snow comes at me,' she chirps." "Chirps"? Tippit: "Gifford talks about everything from her son Cody's diarrhea to her devout Christianity."

The style is terse and bordering on the nasty. The use of Kathie Lee's last name is a feminist touch, although by now the last-name style of writing is traditional in many newspapers. Tippit favors a neat balancing of elements to get over her implied point: the mix of Cody's diarrhea and Kathie Lee's "devout Christianity" is an obvious put-down. Why underline "devout" unless the writer means the opposite, cued cleverly by preceding it with the mention of diarrhea?

Someone in the crowd asks if she does housework. Tippit: "Gifford pauses to think a moment. 'I do toilets, all right? . . . It's like therapy. There is nothing like getting your hands on a good toilet. I mean it.'"

She is asked if she cooks. Tippit: "She wiggles seductively and makes a play on words. 'I really cook. . . . You know what the truth is? . . . I do love to cook. I like to do pasta. I just don't really have a lot of time anymore.'" Tippit goes out of her way to underline Kathie Lee's "seductive wiggle." Why, unless as a put-down to show how coarse (and fake) her "devout Christianity" is.

Somebody hands her a bouquet of flowers.

Tippit's text, quoting Kathie Lee: "'You know what I'm going to do?' she coos. 'I'm going to take these home today on the plane. They're going to do beautifully in my bedroom, and I'm going to ravish my husband tonight.'"

"Coos"? Tippit uses an old-fashioned word out of the nineteen-twenties to paint a portrait.

The interview moves backstage. There Tippit finally inserts an observation in the middle of the piece when she shifts the Qs & As to feminism.

Tippit: "I wonder how a woman with such a busy career [that] she hadn't seen her four-month-old baby and three-year-old son in four days and was heading to a telethon from Orlando balances work and family, which she says is her priority?"

Kathie Lee's response to Tippit's question: "I'm a radical feminists' nightmare because I'm living the opportunity and taking advantage of the opportunities the women's movement has afforded us, and yet I adore my husband, I love God, I'd rather be with my kids than anywhere else and that drives them crazy."

Tippit asks Kathie Lee about her divorce: Did she have any regrets about it?

The text: "'What organization are you from?' she snaps."

An argument ensues in which the spokesperson for Kathie Lee, identified as "Kathie Lee's assistant," says she was told that the interviewer would stick to talk about the clothing line.

Kathie Lee gets in her own comment. "'You know, I'm sure you have an editor or something like that who says, "Go for the jugular, go for the dirt." You know, I'm just really not interested in that, if you don't mind, okay?'"

Tippit: "Gifford's assistant briskly orders me to vacate my chair."

End of interview.

The publication of the story in the weekend magazine section of the paper, *Florida*, elicited a number of letters to the editor. They were pro and con.

Lou Letsinger appreciated Kathie Lee's thoughts and responded in kind. "I certainly hope that the article on Kathie Lee Gifford sets a new tone for some folks in 1994. It was the best feature article for the first 1994 edition of *Florida* magazine because of her remarks on Sarah Tippit's negative questions.

"As I read Kathie Lee's remarks on people going for the dirt, I was yelling out loud, 'Good for her! There need to be more people out there with good Christian values and morals like Kathie Lee!'"

Not all agreed with Letsinger, however. Here's a letter from Rae Anne Campellone:

"Sarah Tippit . . . confirmed my suspicions. Gifford is just another TV personality masquerading as a television journalist.

"Ms. Gifford's comment, 'I thought you were here to talk about the clothes' infuriated me. Any journalist worth their salt knows that when you sit down with a real reporter, you've basically granted them the opportunity to ask any question they might have in mind. The unspoken notion that Gifford could direct the content of our news to her fashion information or curtail any reporters' inquiries about things written about her in the past makes me ill. (Next time, Kathie Lee, just send in a press release and don't waste a good reporter's valuable time on location.)

"I've followed Sarah Tippit's work for years now. She is not spiteful, malicious, or irresponsible in her critiques. From the questions she poses, I can always tell that she's researched her subjects prior to the interviews, and, nine times out of ten, she asks at least two or three questions I would have asked myself.

"In my opinion, she's one of the best human-interest writers in our area."

From the Reverend L. David Harris:

"I appreciated Sarah Tippit's piece on Kathie Lee Gifford.

"I thought Ms. Tippit handled it well, and I hope her experience with Ms. Gifford doesn't discourage her from asking the tough, serious questions. When I first started reading the piece, even though I was/am a fan of Ms. Gifford's, I thought, 'Oh, here we go; another bit of puffery.'

"But Ms. Tippit was different. Ms. Gifford made a mistake when she (and her assistant) didn't treat Ms. Tippit seriously.

"I was a journalist off and on for twenty or more years and worked part of that time as an entertainment columnist. It's tough to deal seriously with personalities because they're looking for softball questions. It must have been an interesting experience for Ms. Tippit."

The story by Sarah Tippit and its aftermath in the letters the article engendered speak volumes about the problems Kathie Lee

Gifford experiences every day when she is on the road and lets herself be interviewed for publicity purposes.

It is her personality and her view on life that are in danger of being questioned and derided. In effect, she is also a target when she performs any of her songs and routines in the entertainment business itself.

For example, on Mother's Day, 1993, Kathie Lee Gifford produced a special titled *Kathie Lee Gifford's Celebration of Motherhood*. It was taped in advance, of course, and shown in prime time at night.

Tom Shales remarked in his critique of the special that Kathie Lee was starting to make Larry King look "like a shrinking violet." He meant that she was in danger of being overexposed—a problem that besets almost any entertainer who makes it big and continues to please the public.

Shales: Setting out to present "a humorous and heartfelt look at motherhood" for Mother's Day, Kathie Lee does deliver one "in the sort of hokey and innocuous way you might expect."

Shales describes cameos by stars like Dolly Parton, Arnold Schwarzenegger, Barbara Walters, Ross Perot, Michael Jordan, Arsenio Hall, Rush Limbaugh, and even Regis Philbin. "These clips," Shales writes, "are horribly edited to melt into one another, sometimes mid-word."

Nevertheless, he says, "A certain sunny affability, most of it radiating from the star, does elevate the proceedings, though the impression lingers that this really should have been a daytime special, not a prime-time hour."

The closing medley of "mom" songs is good, Shales admits, with one exception: "when Gifford sings 'That Face' to a gigantic baby photo of son Cody."

Shales can't help but add: "Gifford reports that at home, Cody has been known to shout, 'Mommy, don't sing!' Perhaps he should assume the role of career adviser."

The piece concludes: "Viewers with limited tolerance of sugary goo are to be warned. Maybe the special should have been advertised this way: 'Kathie Lee Gifford's Celebration of Motherhood: Not for the Squeamish.'"

In December 1994, TV Guide ran a piece entitled "Kathie Lee's Hectic, Harried, and Very Happy Holidays." It was a story revealing her many business interests and several TV productions she was involved in, including a Christmas special that ran in December 1994. It even mentioned the fact that she would be singing the National Anthem at the Superbowl in January 1995. It would be a joint venture with her husband. Frank Gifford, of course, would be covering the Superbowl with his *Monday Night Football* broadcasting crew.

And *TV Guide* got letters.

"Granted," wrote Vivienne Richardson, "Kathie Lee Gifford is a very busy Superlady. But since she doesn't have to shop, cook, wash dishes, bake, do laundry, scrub floors, do windows, vacuum, tend to her children, carpool, and so on, is she really so much more of a dynamo than most mothers? Give me a break—I'd trade places with her any day."

And Terry Linder agreed. "I'm sick and tired of you folks at *TV Guide*. Don't get me wrong—I love your magazine, but I can't take the way you praise people like Kathie Lee Gifford as if she were some sort of goddess. Please—I'm all Kathie Lee'd out!"

When Kathie Lee was invited to participate in the opening ceremonies of Superbowl XXIX, she joined a distinguished troupe of great performers: Garth Brooks, Natalie Cole, Whitney Houston, Cheryl Ladd, Barry Manilow, Wynton Marsalis, Helen O'Connell, Diana Ross, and even the Golden Age film actor Pat O'Brien, who played Knute Rockne to Ronald Reagan's famed "Gipper." (And the singer who performed "The Star-Spangled Banner" at Super Bowl III was Kathie Lee's former mentor, Anita Bryant!)

Kathie Lee Gifford was not new to football openings. At a previous *Monday Night Football* game, when she was five months' pregnant, she sang through the National Anthem and, as she was finishing, she was perturbed to hear an uproar.

"All of a sudden came these horrendous boos," she recalls. "I got my fat body off the field so fast." She felt that the crowd had determined that she was doing something improper for a pregnant woman. Actually, the Bronx cheers were for the visiting team, which had just taken the field.

Kathie Lee learned a lesson from that performance nevertheless. At a football game, as at any public exhibition: "There's an element of disaster present. *Anything* can happen."

15

Regis as Conversationalist:
Reegisms

Regis Philbin has lived his entire life simply paralyzed with fear. Fear he might do the wrong thing. Fear he might fail at this, at that, at anything.

Yet, running counter to the debilitating fear that ruled his life, he nurtured a strong and ever-growing ambition to be better than anyone else at what he was doing. It was, apparently, the clash of these two powerful torments that gave him a remarkable cutting edge—one that provided him with his ability to prick the hypocrisies of the world with a gamin sense of humor that became his trademark.

"The first part of my life I was filled with inhibitions," he once said. "I can't tell you what a struggle it would be to do the sort of thing I do now."

It was fear that helped make him what he became. But it was a fear he kept well hidden within himself. No one knew he was afraid.

He even developed his own psychology of life. "You must

never tell anybody how scared you really are. If you admit it in public, that'll solidify it—cement it in your own mind. But if you fake your way through with others, then it's possible that you can fake yourself out, too. You might just carry your own psyche and think, 'I can do it.' At least you'll give yourself a shot."

A man with an edge of humor in his personality soon learns that he can't do stand-up stuff by himself. With a partner, he's twice as funny. It was partially his life in the service during his navy hitch that taught him the secret of badinage—the Ping-Pong kind of humor that bats ideas back and forth, always building to some kind of ridiculous—and funny—climax.

By the time he began cohosting, rather than hosting, he knew the tricks of the trade, and he certainly made them work for him. And they worked never better than with Kathie Lee—latecomer to the arena in which he was working.

He was always kidding. One day he was bragging to Kathie Lee about a big dinner party he had attended at Saul Steinberg's triplex apartment. Steinberg—the big tycoon.

"He calls me every now and then to pick my brain." Bragging. Grinning. One-upping.

"How long did *that* take?" Kathie Lee shot back.

Then there was the show they did in Chicago in 1993 when Kathie Lee asked the TV audience, "Hey, everybody. We've got about thirty seconds. Do you want to know all there is about Reege's sex life?" Same gag. Different spin.

Not to be outdone, Philbin came right back at her. "Her pals all got to sit up front. My buddies got stuck in the back!"

For sure, it was an "Oh, Reege" moment. Words by the put-upon one. A "Reegism."

While in Chicago they also had the following exchange as they began promoting their upcoming stars:

"We'll do one show live and tape another one at the University of Illinois Pavilion," said Philbin. "We'll have a lot of Chicago personalities with us: Paul Harvey, Siskel and Ebert, Donny

Osmond, who's appearing there, the University of Illinois marching band, Boy George . . ."

Boy George a Chicago personality? the audience wondered. You mean that British singer with the falsetto voice that makes Michael Jackson sound like a bass?

"Sure," said Philbin without batting an eye. "He's a Chicago guy, isn't he?"

"He didn't know Boy George is from England?" Kathie Lee remarked, unable to repress a giggle. "You're lucky he got Boy George's name right. He's a lot smarter than people give him credit for, yet at the same time, he really might not know where Boy George is from."

Philbin is big on *crushing* and *stomping*. They're part of his shtick. In 1991, for instance, he said, "Crushing! Stomping prime time. A little morning show! What does it mean? Stomping the CBS network! Put that down in the *Washington Times*. Let the *Washington Times* illuminate the world. Stomping, crushing, moving and going and . . . you don't care!"

Revealing his humiliations to the public is part of his persona. Unlike other people, when he gets bad seats at a movie premiere he talks about it.

"Some people don't get this thing at all. I have to tell the story whether I had a front-row seat or a last-row seat. I'd never lie because there are maybe a thousand people in the room who saw me sitting behind that pole."

Talk about getting no respect. Even Tom Brokaw disses him. Nobody but Philbin gets dissed by Tom Brokaw. No wonder Philbin wants to stomp and crush.

Nowadays even Kathie Lee is making noises about leaving his show in her search for greener pastures. She grouses occasionally about being bored. It is not the fault of the show at all, and certainly it is not Reege, she says, but she wants to get more opportunities to do some of the other things that are offered to her.

For example, she would love to pursue her singing career much harder than she is pursuing it now. She has had two Broadway opportunities that were hard to say no to.

"She's restless, huh?" Philbin says. "Well, she's gotten very hot commercially. Wow. But I think we both realize that the anchor thing is right here."

As for Philbin, he knows the show is a bona fide success, but he still grouses over the fact that he doesn't make the fifty to eighty million dollars a year that Oprah Winfrey makes with her talk show.

The truth of the matter is that Philbin and Kathie Lee do have a little piece of the action in their show. "So far, no profit, thank you for asking," says Philbin. Of course, everybody around the business assumes they're making a fortune—simply because they're syndicated. But then, so was Arsenio Hall syndicated.

Another of Philbin's gripes is the fact that *Live* isn't aired in the afternoon, but in the morning. Morning is the morgue for television talk shows. More households watch TV in the afternoon than in the morning. Thus *Live* would be getting greater profits.

Why not? After being kicked around live TV for over thirty years, Philbin feels he should be earning more money. TV is his stomping, crushing ground.

However, he retains his modesty. They weren't really a hit even in 1992, when he happened to be grousing for the print medium. They were on the *verge* of being a hit. What was a hit, anyway? Well, Philbin said, a hit was somebody who got a little more national acclaim than Regis and Kathie Lee got.

Actually, Kathie Lee is sick to death of hearing rumors that the reason she doesn't socialize with Regis is because they loathe the sight of one another. Just because they're always at each other's throats on TV doesn't mean they're bitter enemies in real life.

"I love Regis," Kathie Lee claims. "I love him with my whole heart. And after seven years with him I have no itch. I have no desire to be with anyone else. I look forward to being with him every day.

"He just moved into a house about a mile away from us, and I sent him champagne with a note that said, 'There goes the neighborhood.' I adore his wife, Joy. I consider them very close friends."

Regis backs her one hundred percent. "It would make a juicy story, that we don't get along, but the truth is that we've never had a cross word. It's a terrific relationship. I was at the house the other day and played tennis against Frank. Of course, I was beaten." Even when he talks to the press, he's strictly Regis; the Reegisms simply flow from his mouth.

As for Reegisms and how they work, take one morning show just before the flu season in 1994 for a detailed analysis of the comic elements in it—all improv, all off the top of the head.

> "Talk about Frontier Woman," says Regis, eyeballing Kathie Lee's suede coat. "Here she is."
>
> Kathie Lee frowns. "Look at us, though! I can't get over it." She points out the fact that they are both wearing the same kind of outdoor garb.
>
> "I know."
>
> "It's getting to be weird," Kathie Lee decides. "We really don't sleep together and live together and come in together, but somehow we dress alike every day."
>
> "Thank God, we don't!" says Regis, giving the lie to her sarcastic comment.
>
> Kathie Lee looks smug. "You're going to get a shot today," she chants mockingly. "It's gonna hurt your buns. Why don't you get it in your buns just for a change?"
>
> The audience howls. She's talking about a flu shot the two of them are scheduled to have on the show later—as a kind of public service announcement warning of the approaching flu season. Regis looks sick to his stomach. At any moment he will retch.

At this point in the show, even though Regis and Kathie Lee have been sparring with one another in the usual fashion, it becomes obvious that the day's set-to has a theme to it. Flu shots. Nothing could telegraph that fact better than the sudden gleam in Regis's eye, and the manner in which he seems to pick up speed and direction. It is as if suddenly he has gotten on course after a few fumbling attempts at a direction to take.

As for Kathie Lee, she is as aware of Regis's interest and excitement as Regis is himself. And she begins to work toward the role she is going to play against the role that Regis has chosen. What is it to be, she wonders? The stiff-upper-lip hero routine, facing the needle phlegmatically and all that? Or the opposite: the coward in wolf's clothing, finally done in by the tiny needle?

In a moment or two she will know, and when she does, she will follow Regis's lead. And so she stands back and looks Regis up and down.

> "You have a little more meat there than you have in your arm," says Kathie Lee, studying his backside. "It might feel better there. They've gotten it down now so the needle's not even a hair."
>
> "That's right."
>
> "It's the diameter of a hair."
>
> "So, but it still hurts, doesn't it?" Regis asks with an unhappy look.
>
> "Some people have thick hairs."
>
> "Some people," Regis says, glancing at her backside, "have *thick buns!*"
>
> She laughs and bats her eyes at him.

Now Regis's role is becoming a bit clearer. He is going to be Mr. Put-Upon Guy. He is going to suffer in silence and try to stifle the cries of pain. In a comical way, of course. But Kathie Lee now knows which routine they will be following. For her, it is a matter of playing the opposite role. She will be Ms. Frontier Woman Braving the Wilderness. After all, didn't Reege start out kidding her about her frontier costume?

After more badinage, Regis settles on his favorite subject. "Big rating yesterday. Enormous. Eight with a thirty share. Puh-lease." He is awestruck.

"In New York."

He looks at her, annoyed. "In New York." Pause. "Forget it. I mean, I don't even want to talk about it anymore. I don't even know why I brought it up." He puts his hand to his cheek like Jack Benny. "But what a *giant*!"

Soon enough a doctor called "Jay" comes in and prepares to give Regis his flu shot.

A sudden quiet descends on the set. There is imminent suspense. Everybody knows Reege will have some kind of setback when that needle slides in. Will he brave it out? Will he cower and wail? Will he pass out? Not a bad thought, that one—

The doctor puts on surgical gloves like a road company Dr. Kildare. Regis rolls up his sleeve, grimacing.

"Don't you love it when he puts on the gloves?" asks Kathie Lee.

"I *hate* it when you put on the gloves," Regis tells the doctor. "Are the gloves necessary?"

"They're necessary." The doctor is still struggling with them.

"Look how much trouble they are."

"I've never seen him put on gloves before," says Kathie Lee.

Regis is wilting under the strain. "Please, just put the gloves on, will you?" He puts his hands up over his eyes, finding the sight of the gloves being slipped on the doctor's hands an unbearable foreshadowing of the hypodermic pain to follow.

"I like to do this snap," says the doctor, snapping the glove loudly on his hand right in front of Regis's face.

Philbin shies away from the gloved hand, wincing, his hands protecting his face.

182

It is obvious that the doctor has as much ham in him as both Regis and Kathie Lee put together. He is relishing the role. Nevertheless, the routine is taking shape in the classic manner. Improvisation has been with us for centuries. This example is being played by one of today's most skilled and successful teams on TV. The two principals are known to the audience, and the outsider is playing a stereotypical role to which he is adding every nuance he can think of to make the exchange between him and Regis outstanding.

"I like that," says the doctor, referring to his contemptuous glove smack in Regis's face.

"You love it but I hate it," Regis grimaces.

The doctor pulls the shirt up higher on Regis's arm. "Against this enormous muscle here." The doctor knows when to dispense ham as well as aspirins.

Laughter.

"I can't get it up any more!" complains Regis. He means the sleeve any higher on his arm.

"Look at this muscle."

"Really, Reege?" Kathie Lee asks.

A few salacious titters break out in the audience. As the doctor fixes to inoculate Regis, with great mugging on his part, the Notre Dame fight song sounds in the background. Inspired, Regis looks grimly determined to take his medicine. He flexes his muscular arm to the musical riff.

"Go ahead! *Go ahead!*" he shouts at the doctor.

This is comic show biz at its zenith. Here is Regis, playing scaredy-cat all the way, but able to pump himself up into a fake Mohammed Ali because of the Notre Dame fight song, and at the same time quaking in his figurative boots. When he says "Go ahead" he means he wants it over with—fast! So here is muscle beach about to be punctured for good.

183

"Relax. It'll hurt less if you relax."

Regis grits his teeth and rolls his eyes as if he's on the verge of a nervous breakdown. He slides his tongue through his teeth, rolls it around, and the needle goes in.

"Let's hear a round of applause," says the doctor.

"Ew, your blood's in there," says Kathie Lee with undisguised disgust, watching the doctor discard the needle on the table in front of them.

Now Kathie Lee, who is playing the strong silent woman suddenly reverts to her usual role, Madame Sensitiva, cringing at the sight of blood. Good for a laugh.

"It would have been easier without the gloves," says Regis. "I *hate* those gloves, Jay."

"Poor baby," Kathie Lee sympathizes, as if to her son Cody. "Are you okay?"

"Awww," groans the audience in commiseration.

"*Done!*" cries Regis.

"He digs his nails into my hand—" Kathie Lee reports, looking up.

"Jay," says Regis, "you got a little push this time. *Ease it in*, would you?"

"Now, we'll see the difference," says the doctor, making for Kathie Lee, a fresh hypo in hand.

Ahah! The difference! So the doctor has been in on the gag all the time! Anyway, he's playing his role to the hilt. It's up to Kathie Lee now to hang in there and not twitch a muscle. Regis, having no more role to play, comes down off the dramatic high and glances at Kathie Lee teasingly.

"How about a little music for Oral Roberts University!" he suggests.

The Notre Dame fight song blares out again. Regis is nonplussed.

He waves his hand in disgust. "Fine, good, thank you."

"It's too much," Kathie Lee says. "We don't have it in the budget."

"We only have one record up there and that's the Notre Dame fight song."

The doctor plunges the needle into Kathie Lee's arm. She makes a show of yawning in boredom.

The audience roars with laughter.

The yawn is the final insult delivered to Regis from Kathie Lee's quiver of contempt. And of course now the skit is complete. Mr. Scaredy-cat has got his comeuppance and Ms. Tough as Nails has got her revenge for numerous insults. It is definitely tit for tat.

Regis watches her pensively. "Didn't it hurt at all?"

She shakes her head.

"Oh, *stop*! Stop trying to make me out to be a wimp, will you, please?"

"I've given birth twice."

"Reege, you're not a wimp," says the doctor and hands him a lollipop.

Regis looks consoled and unwraps it slowly.

"And for you, too," says the doctor, handing Kathie Lee a lollipop also.

"I'll take hers too," says Regis and snatches it away from the doctor's outstretched hand.

The audience is rolling in the aisles.

And so in the end, Regis comes through exactly as he has been expected to. He not only keeps his own lollipop, but steals Kathie Lee's as well. Not only has every nuance been delivered in the original skeleton of the skit, but new ones have been added by the performers as they went along within the confines of the situation.

There is no truth to the rumor, either, that Regis Philbin and thirty-two-year-old Gelman abhor each other. As he lay dying on the operation table, he thought suddenly, "My gosh, who's gonna finish raising Gelman?"

Philbin never calls Gelman by his first name, Michael, on the show, and he is a constant nettle in Philbin's side. Almost everything about Gelman irks Philbin onstage. One week it will be the length of Gelman's hair, the next it will be something else.

Philbin doesn't even like Gelman to be in his dressing room. Once, when Gelman was modeling comedy wigs in it, Philbin said, "Gelman should be in another room, *but he's made himself at home in here—so what am I gonna do?*"

It's all but impossible for Philbin to finish a sentence without raising his voice as he reaches his conclusion. It's like a wave that keeps building and building as it nears shore and reaches its crescendo when it slams against the beach—"*out of control!*"

Philbin does not lead an ostentatious lifestyle and Gelman is used to flying coach with him, even though they could both easily afford to fly first-class. Philbin has explained, "You will find . . . very few of the usual star trappings around me. I'm a *real person!*"

Philbin doesn't even like riding in stretch limos. They don't fit in with his Joe Six-Pack persona. Recently, when he had to ride in one with a reporter, he told the man, "You're embarrassing me! I'm getting very nervous here!" Philbin prefers a taxi.

As befits him, his fan mail is ordinary. On a typical day he'll get one letter. "Look at the mail pouring in! *When are they gonna leave me alone! What the hell do they want from me?*"

The mystery of Regis's appeal to his audience is a seemingly insoluble one. No one seems to have a clue as to what it is. It's a little like those Russian dolls embedded one in another, and another, and another.

Newsday's David Friedman tried out one theory back in 1988 when he was writing about the show.

"My own hypothesis is that Philbin has a special appeal to women. The appeal of a nonthreatening, nonsexual—but nonetheless macho—male. The kind of man who's sure he's the expert on everything—and loves to complain about people who aren't. Most of all, a man who can talk to women without talking down to them."

Occasionally Regis Philbin will shift gears and change from being put-upon to the braggart. The one thing that he has no compunction about showing off to total strangers are his feet!

"Look at those fabulous arches! Smooth as silk! No long, gnarled toes, not a bunion, not a callus! They're just naturally beautiful!"

Could even Gelman disagree with that?

As an interviewer Regis is as irreverent as he has always been on his talk shows, with the possible exception of the *Joey Bishop* show, in which he played a straight man and did not star as a host. Though he may look like an altar boy, he is anything but, at least when it comes to interviewing his guests—which, to the unsuspecting, can be a surprise.

When he hosted *A.M. Los Angeles* one day he had Julia Child as a guest. During the show she tried to flip an omelet but missed the frying pan. Watching her, Regis pounced.

"Hey, Julia," he said, "why is it on your show you do everything perfectly, but on my show you give us a lousy flip?"

Taken aback, the characteristically unflappable Child stared at him as though she couldn't believe anyone would have the audacity to criticize her expert cooking.

To this day, Regis will nettle his guests in order to save the show from becoming boring. He wants something to happen spontaneously and he knows if he is too polite, nothing interesting is going to develop.

On a *Live With Regis and Kathie Lee* show in November 1994, William Shatner guested and plugged his two books, which Regis promptly claimed Shatner *didn't* write. Put out, Shatner defended himself, saying he did write his book about his *Star Trek* movies. Regis then said he didn't believe Shatner could possibly have any free time to write books, what with his busy acting and producing careers.

As Regis persisted in doubting that Shatner was the author of the books, Shatner became so peeved that he lunged at Regis and pretended he was fixing to wring his neck. Cut to a commercial.

It wasn't mean-spirited grilling. Regis was simply having fun with Shatner, and Shatner was playing along.

Over the years Regis has not changed his technique of interviewing one iota. "This is exactly what I've been doing locally for many years. I knew it would work nationally because it worked in various parts of the country. There's nothing sensational. You have to work at it day after day, so people want to see what you do next. They form a habit."

He did make one change on the *Regis and Kathie Lee* show, according to his own statement. "What's different is I don't know what to do with the trivia question, because in half the country where we're seen on tape, people can't call." Other than that, the show has remained the same type of program he's been doing all along. "I won't change. I'm me. This show is New York. I hope more people love New York because of me and the show."

Supermodel Cindy Crawford recently appeared on the show to a plug a skating extravaganza for the charity of pediatric AIDS. Wearing jeans, boots, and a pricey brown jacket, she told Regis she loves it when he smears Crisco on his neck.

"She does think I'm buff," boasted Regis. "Honest, at Radu's Gym, every now and then I come away from pumping up, you know"—choreographing lifting dumbbells—"and I walk by her." He grimaced and moved his neck, expanding it, ridging the tendons in it, rocking his head from side to side.

"His neck," said Cindy Crawford, watching him. "And he's got Crisco all over his throat."

All worked up, Regis said, "And one day without any, *any* provocation or any solicitation, she said, 'Regis, you're *buff*!'"

Regis had realized that the show was drawing to a halt because the model insisted on talking about her horseback riding adventures. That was just before he introduced the subject of meeting her at the gym where they both work out. It's part of Regis's routine that whenever he has an attractive woman on as a guest he brags about being God's gift to women. It's all part of being the king.

Talk about fear: On Friday, April 7, 1995, Regis was presiding over *Live* without Kathie Lee at his side. She was on vacation from the show for a short period. Christina Ferrare was substituting for her. Regis and Ferrare were chatting with supermodels Naomi Campbell, Elle MacPherson, and Claudia Schiffer about a new restaurant, Fashion Cafe, that the three women were opening up, when the unbelievable happened.

An anonymous telephone caller got the switchboard at WABC-TV studios in Manhattan, and said that he was "from Islam and was a man of peace." He then warned that a bomb would go off inside the building at Columbus Avenue and 67th Street in just thirty minutes. The studio mentioned was the one in which Regis and Christina Ferrare were working.

All six floors of the building were evacuated while the police searched the premises. A prerecorded show with singer Tony Bennett was aired for the balance of the hour.

Meanwhile, the audience of more than a hundred people was shown out the side door, where they stood around in the street waiting to be called back in.

Regis drifted out with the audience and stood there chatting with them. Life had come full circle for him. When he was a neophyte, working that television station in San Diego, he had been forced out of the studio when a bomb scare had interrupted the proceedings and driven everybody out—except for Walter Winchell, who didn't want to let "the ratskies scare" him.

Now that Regis was truly a success, and not just a hard-working novice, here were those telephone phantoms with bombs on their mind once again!

Maybe bomb scares had become a special kind of Reegism—a Reegism, say, that just didn't quite come off.

Regis and his fans were still chatting sometime after 10 A.M. when a limousine pulled up to take him out to the airport for his flight to Florida, where he was scheduled to be that afternoon. When he left, the members of the audience eventually dispersed and went home.

The so-called bomb was never found.

And the show that theater lore says *must go on* never did go on again.

It must be remembered that Regis Philbin had always said he loved it when things went wrong on the set. Somebody up there had obviously heard him.

Or perhaps it was that someone *down there* who knew a good Reegism when he saw it.

16

Kathie Lee as Conversationalist:

Being Kathie Lee

It is an undisputed fact that Kathie Lee Gifford is an eclectic composite of a number of very different personality elements—so much so that it is difficult to define exactly who she is.

Struggling to construct a brief profile on her for *M*—"Life at the Top," as the magazine's subhead reads—writer Barbara Lippert finally had to admit:

"Kathie Lee is an anomaly: a born-again Christian by the age of twelve, she baby-sat for Anita Bryant's children but also opened in Vegas for Shecky Green. She's an evangelical, self-made combination of Barbie and two Marthas (Raye and Stewart). She seems to bring the same evangelical zeal to her relationship with Frank. (To show wifely devotion, her eyes get only slightly less glazed than Nancy Reagan's.)"

At the same time, Lippert admits: "Kathie Lee appeals to people on several levels. First she's got all the nice-girl trappings; she's a really good listener, a really good mother, works for charity and seems to care about other people's children. She sings, she interviews, she decorates, she shops, she gets manicures, she bones up, and she makes a lot of money. But what she clearly excels at is being a wife, in the morning with Regis ('Oh, Reege!') and in the evening with Frank. And it's two very separate spousal styles. Judging from her recent popularity, that's a talent in demand."

Whereas Regis Philbin's interviewing style is flip, Kathie Lee Gifford's comes off as more sanctimonious and unctuous. She is so sincere that she brings tears to her own eyes sometimes, and frequently has to dab the drops off her cheeks.

On one episode of *Live*, when *America's Most Wanted* host was discussing a woman who killed her children by strapping them both in their seat belts while she ran the car off a dock into the bottom of a lake, Kathie Lee looked ill and ran off the stage, to reappear later pale and apologetic.

The critic for *People* magazine said of her interviewing style, "She cannot face anything approximating reality without putting on her oh yucky! face."

Kathie Lee maintains that she is naturally upbeat. She has averred time and again that she would never hurt anybody on purpose or say anything to misrepresent anybody. She truly believes that she has not one evil bone in her body.

In this respect, her interviewing technique is an extension of her personality, which is the reason she is so nice to everybody. It's just that she cannot help it.

As she has put it, more than anything else she wants people to think kindly of her. She is hurt the most by the fact that some people think all she cares about are things that she says don't matter to her a bit—money, houses, jewelry, clothes. She is annoyed that people always make a big deal out of the enormous ring Frank Gifford gave her. It was a multicarat diamond engagement ring that cost the Giff a small fortune—what F. Scott Fitzgerald might have called that "diamond as big as the Ritz."

She frequently waxes sarcastic about the prodigious rock. "I care so darned much about jewelry that until last week I hadn't had it cleaned in two years."

The fact of the matter is that when Kathie Lee did get engaged, she warned her husband-to-be that she only wanted a plain gold ring for her finger. She did not want to be misunderstood and thought to be a gold-digger.

"I'm marrying you because I adore you," she told the Giff. "And I'm not a money-grubbing bitch."

And then the Giff crossed her up by giving her a rock that would knock the eye out of a Turkish pasha. She was upset.

"What happened to my simple gold band?" she asked him.

The Giff smiled. "This isn't for you. It's for your mom and dad. I want them to know how serious I am about you."

That cooled her down a bit. She herself knew that Frank was not teasing her. She realized he was telling her the truth. As for other people—those who never believed that interpretation of the events surrounding the Giff's presentation of the expensive ring to her—they could take it or leave it. Actually, it didn't sound very believable to *anyone*, come to think of it. Kathie Lee is always the first to admit that the story *does* sound far-fetched.

In a somewhat uncharacteristically defensive and apologetic posture, Kathie Lee will explain: "You read a story like this, and you go, 'Yeah, right.' I don't care. It's the truth. That's the way it happened, folks."

This may lead Kathie Lee to begin a little lecture on the times and the mores of the country today. She calls whatever it is that makes people the way they are a "mean-spiritedness" in America. She claims she just doesn't understand it. To her, it's a foreign thing. She was not raised that way.

And she frequently cuts off her lecture at that point and giggles, all the sparks and brightness returning. "I'm giving it to charity anyway!" as she constantly says on *Live* about the big bucks she makes.

How could Kathie Lee ever say anything mean about Frank? To this day she recalls the night he proposed to her.

She can't remember the meal but it happened over dinner. "Who remembers the meal? I wasn't eating. I was in London with

Frank, and we went to a very chic restaurant called Annabelle's. They were very, very booked."

"You'll have to come at eight-thirty," the maitre d' told them. And so they walked around to use up the time, seeing London at its night-life brightest, and came back at exactly eight-thirty and banged and banged on the door.

Nobody would let them in.

Until the maitre d' appeared with his jacket off and his tie loosened well past London standards. Kathie Lee and Frank could see behind the maitre d' and noted that all the people eating in the place were the waiters.

"We were the only people there!" Kathie Lee says. "It's not the least bit chic to show up at Annabelle's at eight-thirty."

There was more to the story. "We went to the bar and spent a long time over a drink, then ordered dinner at ten o'clock."

At that point, they were the only people in the place except for one lone person sitting at the bar. But the atmosphere was total romance. Violinists came around and serenaded them with soft, beautiful music.

"I started sobbing because Frank had not asked me to marry him, though he'd said that day on the radio he was in London with his fiancée."

And so she unloaded on him. "I'm not your fiancée—you haven't asked me." She was Kathie Lee doing Kathie Lee to perfection.

Frank laughed. "Well, we will be married."

As the violinists played on, the waiters came up and joined them. Everybody was listening to the conversation, waiting impatiently for Frank to ask Kathie Lee to marry him.

And so he *did* ask her.

"I finally said yes, and I sobbed the rest of the evening, I was so happy." She pauses. "You know, to this day, I have no idea what I ordered!"

As anyone knows who has ever seen her in person, Kathie

Lee can work the crowd with every bit of the aplomb of Regis Philbin—and in some ways gain even more out of it than the King.

Gail Pennington of the *St. Louis Post-Dispatch* once interviewed her when she was on a personal appearance gig publicizing her clothing line. The temperature in St. Louis that day was approaching 80, and several people in the store had fainted, and were attended to, and yet Kathie Lee was right in the middle of the crowd, chatting with the women who had come to see her and even singing a few bars of "Meet Me in St. Louis" a cappella for them at their request.

The picture was one of dedication and honest camaraderie. For more than an hour and a half, Kathie Lee stood and autographed her picture, was hugged, was photographed with members of the crowd, was shown babies to admire, was told how much her fans loved her and how much they loved *Live*.

She spent several minutes alone with a little girl in a wheelchair, chatting and giving the girl her full attention.

"Some of the people tear my heart out—like that little girl in the wheelchair," Kathie Lee whispered.

A professional newspaper photographer nearby was simply amazed. "She seems to be one of the real ones," he said.

Real enough to know that life is a lot seamier than it appears to be on the surface. And Kathie Lee has always done something about it.

She has often mentioned the fact that the Cody Gifford House and Cassidy's Place were built and maintained to help less fortunate children. "I'm not doing this to be politically correct. If our children can grow up knowing there is a building named after them, designed to save lives or give dying children a quality of love in their lives, then that's the way I know how to impart values to my children.

"I've been in these fields for twenty-eight years. It's like toiling in the vineyard, seeking so little growth, so little return on my investment. All of a sudden I have this major harvest. Now my challenge in this world is What do I put back? What do I give away? I don't want to be conned or be foolish with what riches I've got in life. I want to be wise with them. I've worked too hard to have them wasted. We have truly been blessed. Nobody's going to cry the blues, play their violin, or feel sorry for me. Nor should they. I pinch myself all the time. String me up by my heels if I ever complain."

One of the most awful things that Kathie Lee ever faced was the time the *National Enquirer* came out with a story that her son, Cody, in nursery school had nearly stabbed a little girl's eye with a pair of scissors. She found out that it was an exaggeration; that Cody had poked the child by accident. But because Cody was a "personality" on TV, he was a target for all the gossip writers. Had Kathie Lee been wrong in exposing him in public and to the press as much as she had?

"I look at Cody, and he's so healthy and he's so sweet. He's turned into a wonderful, sweet little human being. So how can I say I did something wrong? But I've learned from my mistakes. I was just too . . . I was so eager to share him because of all the love I'd received from people. I guess I don't feel like I have to do it anymore."

As for her success, "I didn't grow up with a lot of material comfort. My mom sold eggs door-to-door for a little extra money. Frank grew up eating dog food to get by. Neither one of us ever dreamed we'd have this kind of money and success."

About money and success, Kathie Lee is quite articulate. She has said on occasion: "Success is not what your bank account says. It's how wonderful a human being your child is. Where I live is full of people with beautiful homes and tremendous bank accounts who could not tell you right now where their children are."

Money and success notwithstanding, her desire to be nice to everybody she meets carries over to her interviewing technique on *Regis and Kathie Lee*. She goes out of her way to be nice to her guests.

"I realize how much power Reege and I have in a way. I can

either make people's lives a little brighter or be a bitch and put people down and be negative. I think there's enough of that already.

"Most of the mail we get is from people who say, 'Thank you. You start off our day in a nice way.'

"It's not earth-shattering. It's not that I want my tombstone to read: 'She lightened people's loads for an hour a day,' but it's better than 'She ripped people to shreds for a living.' Don't you think?"

The man who has made the most thorough in-depth study of her is her cohost, Regis Philbin. He has hinted there is more to Kathie Lee than one might perceive on first impression. He likes to sum her up this way, as he told Larry King:

"You know, she's just a very spontaneous person. I think she's almost like me. She's got a lot of poise. She had a night-club act for many years before she even got into television, and so she's not afraid to speak her mind. She's got an opinion about everything. She's got a great sense of humor. She's a great-looking lady. I mean, it all comes together."

And that, of course, is the reason the two of them work so well together.

Kathie Lee has admitted that she always had a lot of guilt about slighting either of her children. But when she got together with her own mother, she learned that she was not alone.

"Honey," her mother told her, "even though I was always at home, if you think you had my undivided attention, you're crazy. I was cooking, I was cleaning, I was on the phone, and I had two other children. As long as Cody and Cassidy are happy and well-adjusted, you're doing it right."

Kathie Lee doesn't mind being called upbeat—but she does *resent* being called "perky." To her the old-fashioned word means not having any opinion on anything. After all, she's a very opinionated person, and quite irreverent, too.

Kathie Lee feels that she owes her happiness and success to her parents, especially to her father, who told her, "I love you too much to deny you the privilege of making your own mistakes." The only sin was in not *trying*.

Among her childhood memories was her mother, who would act up on occasion too—much like Kathie Lee. This reminiscence comes from Regis and Kathie Lee's cookbook:

"My mom is great, but she likes to throw things when she gets mad. And she would often get mad at dinnertime. So it was not unusual for a piece of chicken to go flying past you. Or maybe a pork chop would put your eye out if you weren't careful. Somehow most of the food found its way into our stomachs!"

The food that did find its way into Kathie Lee's stomach was superb. "I have great memories of food, because my mom was a fabulous cook. As a special morning treat, she would make us fried bread. I can't imagine anything more artery-clogging or high-fat, but boy, was it delicious!"

And her mom's spaghetti, which was difficult to throw, especially during one of her mother's fits, was out of this world. "Nobody, to this day, makes better spaghetti than my mom!"

About earning money, Kathie Lee has the perfect plan in mind. "I'm not here on earth to amass riches. If God has blessed Frank and me with riches, it is because He knows we will not hoard them or do harm with them, but share them. I don't need my name on one more thing. My biggest concern is still raising my own children."

Marla Maples can understand why Kathie Lee enjoys being at her home in Greenwich, Connecticut. "It's the softest, most romantic home. You go downstairs, and you have this Mickey Mouse-shaped waffle that Frank made on your plate."

During her interviews on the show, Kathie Lee knows her mawkish chattering about Cody and Cassidy can turn some people off. She thanks Regis for saving her bacon when this happens.

She has admitted, "He makes me palatable to certain people who would say, 'Gag!'" when the subject of impossibly cute Cody and impossibly beautiful Cassidy is broached by their doting mother.

She often senses that Regis is about to fire a zinger at her and she retaliates in kind, "before it comes out of his mouth."

In May 1994, Jerry Seinfeld wrote in cameo appearances for Regis Philbin and Kathie Lee Gifford for the last show of the season. In the script, Michael Richards's Kramer character goes on *Live With Regis and Kathie Lee* to promote a new coffee-table book about coffee tables. And, of course, everything got loused up one way or another in typical Seinfeld fashion.

Regis, never happy to be working from a script, tried to focus on the idea. "It's kind of tricky, you know, because you're trying to stay within their boundaries. You don't want to throw them for a loop."

Nevertheless Kathie Lee pointed out that the Seinfeld writers had studied *Live* quite closely and had the dynamics and pacing just right.

"Boy, they've got us down to a T," she said. "And I know it would be done well, and we wouldn't be the object of ridicule. We would be in on the joke, not *the* joke. That's a big, big thing. Nobody's as good at making fun of us as Regis and I are. But humor can't be mean-spirited, to me, to be funny. This was not the least bit mean-spirited. It was just perfect. It captured Kramer. It captured us."

Then there was nothing to it, was there? someone asked.

"Hey," Kathie Lee responded. "We were 'nothing' before they were 'nothing,' and you can quote me on that. We own nothingness. Nothingness is ours. We're happy for everybody else's success, but let's give credit where credit is due."

Kenneth R. Clark in the *Chicago Tribune* gave a rundown of an early-morning segment on *Live* with Kathie Lee in fine fettle. He described her bright-eyed and bushy-tailed appearance one morning during the famous host chat. He pointed out that she had gone to a banquet the night before where Regis Philbin was being honored by the Irish Chamber of Commerce.

But what struck Kathie Lee's eye was the wife of one of the

delegates. She was a woman of what a conservative journalist might describe as "generous endowment."

"You should have *seen* her!" Kathie Lee mugged to the audience. At the same time she waved her hands in the air very suggestively and opened her eyes wide as if viewing something not of this world.

It was Regis who tried to save the day. He snatched up a copy of the *New York Post*—one of the tabloids he frequently reads and derides on camera—and began flipping through to the baseball section, immediately beginning a monologue about baseball and its many virtues and vices.

Kathie Lee did not take offense. If anything, she basked in Regis's antics. She continued to stare out at the audience in disbelief at what she had seen the night before. The audience in turn was absolutely in the aisles with laughter. Regis finally shook his head in a kind of parody of dismay as Kathie Lee sat there beaming out at America.

Clark: "You won't find such [a dialogue] on the *Today Show* or *CBS This Morning* or *Good Morning America*."

In 1995, Kathie Lee surprised everybody with yet another book, this one coauthored with five-year-old Cody Gifford, her son. It was called *Listen to My Heart: Lessons in Love, Laughter, and Lunacy* and was cast in the form of a series of "conversations with Cody." The conversations covered a great deal of ground— small, trivial things, monumental thoughts, philosophies, concepts of one kind or another.

Somehow, even the small things in the book tend to linger in the mind and become larger in retrospect. In one instance, Kathie Lee writes that she feels she is beginning to sound just like her own mother. It's the orders she's giving Cody and the way she's looking out for him. Then she switches mood and daydreams that her own children will feel about her the way she feels now about her mother.

And then, the key phrase: except two times.

Two times Kathie Lee's mother failed to arrive at home before

200

Kathie Lee did from school. And she had no key to get in the house. And so, when anyone asks her if her mother was perfect, she always says: "Yes, except for two times."

And the kicker: "But remind me to give my kids their own keys."

It's simple, but precise. The feeling is there. The idea is there.

Publishers Weekly, the trade magazine for the publishing industry, reviewed the book and gave it a mildly plus review. "Much of the dialogue," the reviewer admitted, "is hopelessly cute (Cody to Mom: 'Monsieur, I am Grey Poupon. I poop on this, I poop on that, I poop on everything'), but some is surprisingly clever and even thought-provoking." The reviewer calls it "a short and sugary Mother's Day treat for Gifford fans." Proceeds from the book, incidentally, went to the Cody Foundation for Cassidy's Place, the home located in New York City for children with HIV and AIDS.

Regis Philbin was a seasoned professional in the talk-show host business when he met Kathie Lee Johnson. He had shared his hosting job with a number of other women cohosts. Yet within months after she had joined him and the two were beginning to make sparks in the bleak morning firmament it was obvious that she was giving Regis something that none of his other partners had.

What she gave him, and still gives him, is *youth*. It was Regis himself who said of her: "She even makes David Hartman look young!"

She also *throws* just enough sass in his face when he goes on one of his put-upon grinchlike tirades.

But she possesses another quality that helps make Regis even better than he is. She really enjoys his sense of humor. For many women, it is a difficult thing to laugh and enjoy a man's particular brand of humor. Yet Regis Philbin sometimes actually breaks up Kathie Lee. And it is honest stuff.

In addition to laughing at his jokes, Kathie Lee knows the

secret of good comedy. She laughs at herself before anyone else can beat her to it.

Yet what Kathie Lee gives Regis Philbin is only half the story. What Regis gives her is something else again. Kathie Lee is a mistress of the irrepressible put-down. In return Regis offers the deadpan look that could kill.

Quite frequently Kathie Lee strays over that thin line that divides the tasteful from the tasteless. But she can say awful things because she has an inner dignity that balances her unbelievable mouth. In addition, it is Regis who uses everything at his command—body language, words, actions—to let her know that she's done it again. By acting the aggrieved male, he turns the crowd against *him*, and lets her fly on unaffected.

Kathie Lee can be as strong as she wants every so often, just to remind people that she has a way with words, that she sizes up people just as astutely as Regis, that she believes in letting everyone know exactly how she feels about—well—everything!

Basically, this pair is playing the age-old comedy of the sexes. But their *Kiss Me Kate* dialogue has a nice new flavor to it. It's their humor, usually missing from such encounters, that makes them different. And the humor of each of the cohosts is so different and so unique that it never seems to repeat itself.

The combination makes for a winning pair of talk-show hosts and a show that is *real*.

Index

In an extraordinary book that transcends sports biography, Bob Greene takes the reader along with Jordan over two seasons with the Chicago Bulls, during glorious championship surges and trying personal moments. With rare insight, Greene reveals the person inside the icon: a man who makes millions but cannot go for a quiet walk around the block without getting mobbed, a man who competes ferociously on the court, but who performs some of his most remarkable and unexpected feats away from the limelight.

HANG TIME

BOB GREENE

"Jordan seems to open up more to Greene than anybody."
—Mike Lupica, New York *Daily News*

He was a charming hitchhiker with a body to die for in *Thelma and Louise*. He was the sensuous undead in *Interview with the Vampire*. And in *Legends of the Fall*, his first big romantic lead, he was simply drop-dead gorgeous. How did a sensitive Missouri boy end up as the male sex symbol of the 1990s?

It's time to get a closer look at the real Brad Pitt— an irresistible mix of hellraiser and choir boy who dropped out of college just two credits short of graduating to head for Hollywood.

Packed with lots of details, and 16 irresistible pages of photos, Chris Nickson's stunning biography is the best way to get into Brad Pitt's world.

Go behind the scenes into the life and career of Hollywood's sexiest hunk

BRAD PITT

CHRIS NICKSON

— Coming in October 1995 —

_____ 95727-0 $4.99 U.S./$5.99 Can.

His inventive, off-the-wall humor made America laugh out loud in movies like *Big, Turner and Hooch*, and *A League of Their Own*. His charm and boyish good looks won over Darryl Hannah in *Splash* and Meg Ryan in *Sleepless in Seattle*. His genius for breathing life into a character made *Forrest Gump* a household name. And his haunting Oscar-winning performance in *Philadelphia* established him as one of today's hottest leading men.

Warm, witty and vulnerable, Tom Hanks is both the everyman we can all identify with and an actor with stunning star quality. Now, Roy Trakin traces Hanks' life and career in this honest, no-holds-barred biography.

TOM HANKS
JOURNEY TO STARDOM

ROY TRAKIN

There Will Never Be a Book on Streisand This Intimate . . .
until She Writes One Herself.

There has never been a star like Barbra Streisand—an artist of uncompromising vision who combines explosive flashes of talent with monumental outbursts of ego. Cold, brash, obsessively controlling, vain, insecure, devastatingly shy, she can also be sensual, warm, funny, and sizzling with sex appeal. But who is the real Streisand?

In this fascinating book, acclaimed biographer Randall Riese reveals all the faces of Barbra—plus behind-the-scenes insights into Barbra's personal life. It's Barbra as you've never seen her before.

Her Name Is
BARBRA

Randall Riese

"SIZZLING!"
—*New York Post*

HER NAME IS BARBRA
Randall Riese
_____ 95391-7 $6.99 U.S./$7.99 Can.